The Short Path to
ENLIGHTENMENT

The Short Path to Enlightenment is a deeply supportive text from the extraordinary Paul Brunton, the spiritual explorer who first brought knowledge of Ramana Maharishi to the West. In this work published by the Paul Brunton Philosophic Foundation, readers receive the invitation and instruction to discover the truth of oneself. The accompanying excellent glossary gives depth of understanding to Brunton's unique terminology. This book is alive with supreme knowledge. May it support you in immediately and continually recognizing yourself.   **—Gangaji**

In *The Short Path to Enlightenment,* Paul Brunton gives voice to the profound teachings of immediate spiritual awakening that have the power to short circuit the seeker in us and reveal the true nature of reality here and now. But the true gift of this wonderful book is in how nuanced and subtle Paul Brunton understood these profound and transformational teachings and how directly he conveys them. Read this book as you would a scripture or a sutra and let it open your eyes to eternity.   **—Adyashanti**

Paul Brunton needs no introduction to our readers. The value of his insights is that they come from a long and sustained journey by someone whose intelligence, perseverance and integrity are self-evident. There is an element of common sense coupled with a refined fluency in his writing style which is immediately engaging. A gifted writer, his books published in the 1930s, 40s and 50s, are classics and have quietly influenced generations of seekers. Through his books, especially his *A Search in Secret India* many especially in the West came to know of Ramana Maharshi. Paul Brunton has the ability not just to inspire but clarify what is essential. The simplicity of his writing veils the sophistication of his comprehension. These short selections on a wide range of spiritual topics are meant more for meditation than browsing.

—*The Mountain Path Journal*
the publication of the Ramana Ashram

The Short Path to
ENLIGHTENMENT

Instructions for
Immediate Awakening

PAUL BRUNTON

Compiled by Mark Scorelle & Jeff Cox

For the
Paul Brunton Philosophic Foundation by

Larson Publications
Burdett, New York

ISBN-10: 1-936012-39-1
SBN-13: 978-1-936012-39-8
eISBN 13: 978-1-936012-40-4
Library of Congress Control Number: 2023937547

Publisher's Cataloging-In-Publication Data
(Provided by Cassidy Cataloguing Services, Inc.)

Names:	Brunton, Paul, 1898-1981, author.	Scorelle, Mark, compiler.	Cox, Jeff, 1947- compiler.	Paul Brunton Philosophic Foundation.
Title:	The short path to enlightenment : instructions for immediate awakening / Paul Brunton ; compiled by Mark Scorelle & Jeff Cox.
Description:	Expanded second edition.	Burdett, New York : Larson Publications : Published for the Paul Brunton Philosophic Foundation, [2023]	Includes bibliographical references.
Identifiers:	ISBN: 978-1-936012-39-8 (print)	978-1-936012-40-4 (ebook)	LCCN: 2023937547
Subjects:	LCSH: Enlightenment (Buddhism)	Spiritual life.	Philosophy, Indic.	BISAC: RELIGION / Spirituality.	BODY, MIND & SPIRIT / Inspiration & Personal Growth.
Classification:	LCC: BL629.5.E5 B78 2023	DDC: 181.4--dc23

Published for the Paul Brunton Philosophic Foundation
by Larson Publications
4936 NYS Route 414
Burdett, New York 14818 USA
larsonpublications.com

32 31 30 29 28 27 26 25 24 23
10 9 8 7 6 5 4 3 2 1

Contents

Preface to the Second Edition

AMONG the wide variety of spiritual techniques in the world's mystical traditions, one can find the threads of a very simple—yet powerful—approach to spiritual awakening. This method is variously called the Direct Path, Non-dualism, Mahamudra, Dzogchen, Advaita and other names, depending on the specific spiritual tradition in which it is rooted. Paul Brunton refers to it as the Short Path. And he uses the term *Overself* for the Reality that we are.

In the West, there is increasing interest in Short Path teachings. The directness of the path, its pointing at the Real that is always and already here, its lack of jargon, and its consonance with the discoveries of cutting-edge physics and other sciences help make it particularly relevant for our times.

Many contemporary teachers trace their lineage to the great Indian sage Ramana Maharshi. In fact, it was Paul Brunton who first introduced Ramana to the West through his best-selling *A Search in Secret India,* published in the 1930s.

Brunton's many books not only describe the Short Path, but place it in the context of the whole range of spiritual endeavor, including the important development on the Long Path of reason and ethics, purification of the emotions, concentration, and so forth. His extraordinarily knowledgeable and broad view helps orient spiritual seekers, so they can discern how the Short

Path dovetails with mystical practices with which they might be familiar.

During the years following the original 2014 publication of *The Short Path to Enlightenment*, we recognized the need to include other writings about the Short Path method and philosophy, ones that are key elements important to the realization that the Short Path offers. These topics include: the power of grace and surrender, the opening of the heart to the Overself as one aspires to practice the Short Path, and the need to embody a joyful attitude as one engages in the Short Path.

May this book be the spark that ignites the fire of immediate awakening!

Blessings on your journey.
Paul Brunton Philosophic Foundation
www.PaulBrunton.org
www.PBarchives.org

Introduction

As I think back, I can see that the seed for this project was planted with meeting Paul Brunton in 1977. The aura of peace, clarity and emptiness that surrounded him gave me a tangible clue of the goal of this spiritual quest.

After his death in 1981, *The Notebooks of Paul Brunton* were published in sixteen volumes; in them I read with interest the advanced contemplation material on the short or direct path. It was with great pleasure that I picked up the thread of enlightenment, self-realization and non-dual teachings in those books.

I also came across 1,200 pages of Brunton's notes on the teachings of V. Subrahmanya Iyer; a small volume came out of that material, entitled *Advaita: The Truth of Non-Duality*. Later, my interest turned to the modern exponents of the enlightenment teachings: Eckhart Tolle, Gangaji, Adyashanti, and many others. I started an e-mail list (Wisdom-l@yahoogroups.com) to promote awareness and discussion of the parallels between Brunton's teachings and the flood of material that has come out in the last twenty years.

This small book consists of a selection of paragraphs written by Brunton, many of which were posted over the last fifteen years to that e-mail list. (Each paragraph is followed by a numerical reference to *The Notebook* category from which it was taken.)

I hope you enjoy these gems and find reading them as enlightening as I do.

Today, the number of people who have some kind of deep insight into Reality is remarkable. This is partially due to the availability of teachings that were buried for centuries in the ashrams of India and the temples of Tibet, Japan, and Southeast Asia. Brunton played no small part in researching, exploring and presenting these teachings to the Western spiritual audience in the twentieth century. And he still has a lot to offer: his rational, sane, yet deep and profound insights along the path are invaluable and point out errors and misunderstandings that could lead the seeker astray. For this we thank him and offer this book in some small measure of gratitude.

It is said—and I think there is some truth to it—that fifty percent of accomplishing the path to enlightenment is simply finding out that it is a real possibility. And it doesn't necessarily take countless incarnations spent in service, purification and practices, as some of the ancient traditions say. The realization is virtually here now; a simple recognition, a brief moment of grace, could make it actual. Perhaps this moment may come to you from reading these pages.

Special thanks to Jeff Cox and Sam Cohen for adding additional quotes and for helping to organize the paragraphs into thematic chapters.

Mark Scorelle

March 2012

A Note to the Reader

"The most precious thing which anyone could find cannot be given to others. Spirit is incommunicable and impalpable. But words, which tell about it, can be given to them."

(12-4-110)

PAUL BRUNTON was well aware that the Western mind found repetition tiresome. But when it came to imparting spiritual understanding, he considered the Eastern mind to be wiser. Teachers of great truths throughout the ancient world found it invaluable. ". . . the more important tenets of higher philosophy are intellectually extremely subtle, so subtle as not to be apparent at first contact with them, and extremely difficult to realize. The repeated contact with them, however, acts as a kind of indirect meditation and removes their unfamiliarity, renders them understandable, and causes them little by little to sink into the emotional consciousness." (8-5-114)

Thus, to enable readers to more easily give inner life to the subtle meanings in his words, and to deepen one's understanding of them, Paul Brunton uses a presentation which is unique to the Western mind. He puts his thoughts into short notes. At first reading one gets the idea but perhaps only at a superficial level. Subsequent quotes, although somewhat repetitious, come from a slightly different slant, moving the readers' attention around a seed thought in a circular fashion. The quotes interact, illuminating each other. Each quote can be used in a contemplative way, serving to deepen awareness, arouse the readers' intuition and bring them closer to their precious inner spirit.

Each selection in *The Short Path to Enlightenment* ends with its location in *The Notebooks of Paul Brunton*. The source category, chapter, and paragraph number are indicated for each selection to facilitate further study of the topics (see paulbrunton. org/notebooks/). Please note that the editors, not Paul Brunton, determined the sequence of material in this book.

Terms created by Paul Brunton such as Overself and World-Mind, and a few foreign terms may not be familiar to the reader. A glossary is provided at the end of the book. Each term is explained using quotes from *The Notebooks*.

Paul Brunton wrote in the mid twentieth-century when the literary convention was to use "he" rather than "he or she," but certainly he intended these teachings for everyone drawn to study them.

Two THINGS have to be learned in this quest. The first is the art of mind-stilling, of emptying consciousness of every thought and form whatsoever. This is mysticism or Yoga. The disciple's ascent should not stop at the contemplation of anything that has shape or history, name or habitation, however powerfully helpful this may have formerly been to the ascent itself. Only in the mysterious void of Pure Spirit, in the undifferentiated Mind, lies his last goal as a mystic. The second is to grasp the essential nature of the ego and of the universe and to obtain direct perception that both are nothing but a series of ideas which unfold themselves within our minds. This is the metaphysics of Truth. The combination of these two activities brings about the realization of his true Being as the ever beautiful and eternally beneficent Overself. This is philosophy. (20-4-134)

What Is the Short Path?

THE SHORT PATH offers the quickest way to the blessings of spiritual joy, truth, and strength. For since these things are present in the Overself, and since the Overself is present in all of us, each of us may claim them as his own by the direct declaration of his true identity. This simple act requires him to turn around, desert the dependence on personal self, and look to the original Source whence flows his real life and being, his true providence and happiness. Disregarding all contrary ideas that the world outside thrusts upon him, disdaining the ego's emotions and desires concerning them, he "prays without ceasing" to that Source. That is, he keeps himself concentrated within upon it until he can feel its liberating qualities and expand in its sunny glories.   (23-1-60)

What is the key to the Short Path? It is threefold. First, stop searching for the Overself since it follows you wherever you go. Second, believe in its Presence, with and within you. Third, keep on trying to understand its truth until you can abandon further thoughts about it. You cannot acquire what is already here. So drop the ego's false idea and affirm the real one.   (23-1-92)

The other part of the answer is that the Overself is always here as man's innermost truest self. It is beginningless and endless in time. Its consciousness does not have to be developed as something new. But the person's awareness of it begins in time and has to be developed as a new attainment. The ever-presence of Overself means that anyone may attain it here and now. There is no inner necessity to travel anywhere or to anyone in space or to wait years in time for this to happen. Anyone, for instance, who attends carefully and earnestly to the present exposition may perhaps suddenly and easily get the first stage of insight, the lightning-flash which affords a glimpse of reality, at any moment. By that glimpse he will have been uplifted to a new dimension of being. The difficulty will consist in retaining the new perception. For ancient habits of erroneous thinking will quickly reassert themselves and overwhelm him enough to push it into the background. This is why repeated introspection, reflective study, and mystical meditation are needed to weaken those habits and generate the inner strength which can firmly hold the higher outlook against these aggressive intruders from his own past.

(22-3-24)

The Overself is not a goal to be attained but a realization of what already is. It is the inalienable possession of all conscious beings and not of a mere few. No effort is needed to get hold of the Overself, but every effort is needed to get rid of the many impediments to its recognition. We cannot take hold of it; it takes hold of us. Therefore the last stage of this quest is an effortless one. We are led, as children by the hand, into the resplendent presence. Our weary strivings come to an abrupt end. Our lips are made shut and wordless.   (22-3-9)

"Be still and know that I am God" is the key to the enigma of truth, for it sums up the whole of the Short Path. Paradox is the final revelation. For this is "non-doing." Rather is it a "letting-be," a non-interference by your egoistic will, a silencing of all the mental agitation and effort.   (23-5-202)

The Short Path is the real way! All else is mere preparation of the equipment for it. For with it he is no longer to direct his meditation upon the shortcomings and struggles of the personal self but up to the Overself, its presence and strength. For the consciousness of the Real, the True, the Beneficent and Peaceful comes by its Grace alone and by this practice he attracts the visitation. (23-1-102)

The Short Path uses (a) *thinking*: metaphysical study of the Nature of Reality; (b) *practice*: constant remembrance of Reality during everyday life in the world; (c) *meditation*: surrender to the thought of Reality in stillness. You will observe that in all these three activities *there is no reference to the personal ego*. There is no thinking of, remembering, or meditating upon oneself, as there is with the Long Path. (23-1-98)

This notion that we must wait and wait while we slowly progress out of enslavement into liberation, out of ignorance into knowledge, out of the present limitations into a future union with the Divine, is only true if we let it be so. But we need not. We can shift our identification from the ego to the Overself in our habitual thinking, in our daily reactions and attitudes, in our response to events and the world. We have thought our way into this unsatisfactory state; we can unthink our way out of it. By incessantly remembering what we really are, here and now at this very moment, we set ourselves free. Why wait for what already is? (23-1-1)

The idea that we have to wait for liberation from the ego and enlightenment by the Overself, to evolve through much time and many reincarnations, is correct only if we continue to remain mesmerized by it, but false if we take our stand on reality rather than appearance: we are now as divine as we ever shall be—but we must wake up from illusion and see this truth.   (23-1-25)

What the Japanese Zenists call "The Sudden Path" and the Tibetan Sages "The Short Path" are closely similar in important points. Both prescribe that the work be done in a joyful attitude. Both teach that the goal is also the means. Both claim to offer a rocket flight to Reality.   (23-5-120)

On the Long Path he identifies himself with the personal ego, even though it be the higher part of the ego, whereas on the Short Path he is only the observer of the ego. This shows up clearly in his attitudes. "What have I to do with my personal past?" he asks himself on the second path. "That belongs to a dead self, which is now rejected and with which I refuse to identify."

(23-5-81)

In the early stages of enlightenment, the aspirant is overwhelmed by his discovery that God is within himself. It stirs his intensest feelings and excites his deepest thoughts. But, though he does not know it, those very feelings and thoughts still form part of his ego, albeit the highest part. So he still separates his being into two—self and Overself. Only in the later stages does he find that God not only is within himself but is himself.   (23-7-300)

Recognition is a prominent feature on the Short Path. The Overself is always there but only those on the Short Path recognize this truth and think accordingly. The world is always with us, but only those on the Short Path recognize the miracle that it is. In moments of exaltation, uplift, awe, or satisfaction—derived from music, art, poetry, landscape, or otherwise—thousands of people have received a Glimpse; but only those on the Short Path *recognize* it for what it really is. (23-1-114)

So the Short Path has begun. It makes life considerably pleasanter because you are supposed to make a 180 degree turn, putting your past behind you, looking first on the bright side, the sunny side, of your spiritual life. Very often a glimpse is given which starts you off on the Short Path, and you are shown what to do. You get new exercises, or no exercise at all. You see things which you missed before when you just saw the gloomy side. The exercises may be chosen by the seeker or by the guru. Each must find his own, but all are bright, cheerful, constructive.

(excerpted from 23-5-56)

It is a matter of transferring attention for this brief period from the ego and fixing it lovingly on the Overself. For while thought dwells in and on the ego alone, it is kept prisoner, held by the little self's limitations, confined in the narrow circle of personal affairs, interests, problems. The way out is this transfer of attention. But the change needs a motive power, a push. This comes from love and faith combined—love, aspiration, longing for Overself, and faith in its living ever-presence within. (4-2-287)

He is to keep the thought of the goal itself continually before him, to give the mental consciousness as its principal occupation a meditation on the Overself. This is the basis of Short Path work and this is why, before he can hope to succeed, he must first have set himself the Long Path task of gaining some control over his thoughts. (23-4-20)

Because the Short Path is an attempt to withdraw from the ego's shade and to stand in the Overself's sunshine, it must be accompanied by the deliberate cultivation of a joyous attitude. And because it is so largely a withdrawal from the Long Path's disciplines, it must also be accompanied by a sense of freedom. Hence its proper physical facial expression is the radiant smile. Its votary should look for beauty and seek to come into harmony at all times—in Nature, in art, in the world, and in himself.

(23-6-55)

Most people who start the short path have usually had a glimpse of the Overself, because otherwise they find it too difficult to understand what the short path is about. The long path, through its studies and practices, is the period of preparation for the advanced quest. It is called the long path because there is much work to be done on it and much development of character and emotions to go through. After some measure of this preparation the aspirants enter the short path to complete this work. This takes a comparatively much shorter time and, as it has the possibility of yielding the full self-enlightenment at any moment, it ends suddenly. What they are trying to do on the long path continues by itself once they have entered fully on the short path. On the long path they are concerned with the personal ego and as a result give the negative thoughts their attention. On the short path they refuse to accept these negatives and instead look to the Overself. Thus the struggles will disappear. This change of attitude is called "voiding" them. The moment such negative ideas and feelings appear, then instead of using the long path method of concentrating on the opposite kind of thought, such as calmness instead of anger, the short path way simply drops the negative idea into the Void, the Nothingness, and forgets it. Now such a change can only be brought about by doing it quickly and firmly and turning to the Overself. Constant remembrance of the Overself has to be done all the way through the short path. The long path works on the ego; but the short path uses the result of that work, which prepared them to come into communion with the Overself and become receptive to its presence, which includes its grace. In order to understand the short path, it might be helpful to compare it to the long path which consists of a series of exercises and efforts which gradually develops concentration and character and knowledge. But the long path does not lead to the goal. On the long path you often measure your own progress. It is an endless path because there will always be new circumstances which bring new temptations and trials and confront the aspirant with new challenges. No matter how spiritual the ego becomes it does not enter the whitest light, but remains in the greyish light. On the long path you must deal with the urges of interference arising from the lower self and the negativity which enters from the surrounding environment. But the efforts on the long path will at last invoke the grace, which opens the perspective of the short path.

The short path is not an exercise but an inner standpoint to invoke, a state of consciousness where one comes closer or finds peace in the Overself. There are, however, two exercises which can be of help to lead to the short path, but they have quite a different character than the exercises on the long path. The short path takes less time because the aspirant turns around and faces the goal directly. The short path means that you begin to try to remember to live in the rarefied atmosphere of the Overself instead of worrying about the ego and measuring its spiritual development. You learn to trust more and more in the Higher Power. On the short path you ignore negativity and turn around 180 degrees, from the ego to the Overself. The visitations of the Overself are heralded through devotional feeling, but also through intuitive thought and action. Often the two paths can be treaded simultaneously, but not necessarily equally.

Often the aspirant is not ready to start these two exercises until after one or several glimpses of the Overself.

The "remembrance exercise" consists of trying to recall the glimpse of the Overself, not only during the set meditation periods but also in each moment during the whole working span of the day—in the same way as a mother who has lost her child can not let go of the thought of it no matter what she is doing outwardly, or as a lover who constantly holds the vivid image of the beloved in the back of his mind. In a similar way, you keep the memory of the Overself alive during this exercise and let it shine in the background while you go about your daily work. But the spirit of the exercise is not to be lost. It must not be mechanical and cold. The time may come later when the remembrance will cease as a consciously and deliberately willed exercise and pass by itself into a state which will be maintained without the help of the ego's will.

The remembrance is a necessary preparation for the second exercise, in which you try to obtain an immediate identification with the Overself. Just as an actor identifies with the role he plays on the stage, you act *think* and live during the daily life "as if" *you* were the Overself. This exercise is not merely intellectual but also includes feeling and intuitive action. It is an act of creative imagination in which by turning directly to playing the part of the Overself you make it possible for its grace to come more and more into your life. (23-5-2)

Once we become conscious of this truth the scales fall from our eyes. We give up our bondage to the erroneous belief in limitation. We refuse to entertain this false thought that there is some lofty condition to be attained in the far future. We are resolute that the Self shall recognize itself *now*. For what shall we wait?

Let us stack all our thoughts upon the Reality, and hold them there as with a spike; it will not elude us, and the thoughts will dissolve and vanish into air, leaving us alone with the beauty and sublimity of the Self.   (23-5-204)

In this moment here and now, letting go of past and future, seeking the pure consciousness in itself, and not the identifications it gets mixed up with and eventually has to free itself from—in this moment he may affirm his true being and ascertain his true enlightenment without referring it to some future date.

(24-3-256)

It is objected, why search at all if one really is the Overself? Yes, there comes a time when the deliberate purposeful search for the Overself has to be abandoned for this reason. Paradoxically, it is given up many times, whenever he has a Glimpse, for at such moments he knows that he always was, is, and will be the Real, that there is nothing new to be gained or searched for. Who should search for what? But the fact remains that past tendencies of thought rise up after every Glimpse and overpower the mind, causing it to lose this insight and putting it back on the quest again. While this happens he must continue the search, with this difference, that he no longer searches blindly, as in earlier days, believing that he is an ego trying to transform itself into the Overself, trying to reach a new attainment in time by evolutionary stages. No! through the understanding of the Short Path he searches knowingly, not wanting another experience since both wanting and experiencing put him out of the essential Self. He thinks and acts as if he is that Self, which puts him back into It. It is a liberation from time-bound thinking, a realization of timeless fact.   (23-6-110)

As he advances in the idea of being detached from results and possessions, he will inevitably have to advance in the idea of being detached from concern about his own spiritual development. If he is to relinquish the ego, he will also have to relinquish his attempts to improve it. This applies just as much to its character as to its ideas. (24-3-200)

One thing about the Short Path which must be firmly impressed on the student's mind is that its success depends on how much love for its objective a man brings to it. If he has ever had a moment's Glimpse of the Overself, and has fallen more deeply in love with it than with anything else, he will be able to fulfil the basic requirement for all Short Path techniques: but without such wholehearted attachment, he is sure to fail. (23-1-90)

When a man consciously asks for union with the Overself, he unconsciously accepts the condition that goes along with it, and that is to give himself wholly up to the Overself. He should not complain therefore when, looking forward to living happily ever after with a desired object, that object is suddenly removed from him and his desire frustrated. He has been taken at his word. Because another love stood between him and the Overself, the obstruction had to be removed if the union were to be perfected; he had to sacrifice the one in order to possess the other. The degree of his attachment to the lesser love was shown by the measure of his suffering at its being taken away; but if he accepts this suffering as an educator and does not resent it, it will lead the way to true joy. (18-4-138)

The central point of this quest is the inner opening of the ego's heart to the Overself. (1-1-3)

Saint John of the Cross gave the following advice: "Enter into your heart and labour in the presence of God who is always present there to help you. *Fix your loving attention upon Him without any desire to feel or hear anything of God.*" Could a beginner be asked to apply such words? A person in a well-advanced state is alone likely to respond to them. Or, those who have been told about the Short Path and have studied its nature and tried to fit it into their inner work—whether they be beginners or proficient—can also put them into practice. (23-1-66)

While giving all attention to the Overself, or to its remembrance, or to its various aspects, or to the idea of it, he forgets himself. This makes it possible to transcend the ego. And this is why the Short Path *must* be travelled if the preparatory work of the other Path is to be completed. (23-4-2)

The man who thinks of himself instead of the Overself when practising a Short Path exercise, who is unable to forget his little ego, is a traitor to that Path. (23-2-48)

This is the wonder of the Short Path—that it teaches us to refuse at once every thought which seeks to identify us with the feeble and unworthy self. This is the gladness of the Short Path—that it urges us to accept and hold only those thoughts which identify us directly with the strong and divine Overself, or which reflect its goodness and wisdom. (23-1-143)

If each attack of adverse force, each temptation that tries a weakness, is instantly met with the Short Path attitude, he will have an infinitely better chance of overcoming it. The secret is to remember the Overself, to turn the battle over to IT. Then, what he is unable to conquer by himself, will be easily conquered *for him* by the higher power. (6-1-68)

On the Short Path, instead of attacking the lower self, he lifts himself up to the presence of the higher. The evil in him may then melt away of its own accord. (23-1-132)

The Short Path provides him with the chance of making a fresh start, of gaining new inspiration, more joy. (23-1-180)

This is the concept which governs the Short Path: that he is in the Stillness of central being all the time whether he knows it or not, that he has never left and can never leave it. And this is so, even in a life passed in failure and despair. (23-1-8)

The more he practises identifying himself with the timeless Now (not the passing "now"), the more he works for true freedom from besetting passions and dragging attachments. This is the Short Path, more heroic perhaps but in the end much pleasanter than the Long Path. (23-5-217)

Why should the Short Path be a better means of getting Grace than the Long one? There is not only the reason that it is not occupied with the ego but also that it continually keeps up remembrance of the Overself. It does this with a heart that gives, and is open to receive, love. It thinks of the Overself throughout the day. Thus, it not only comes closer to the source from which Grace is being perpetually radiated, but it also is repeatedly inviting Grace with each loving remembrance. (23-6-149)

It is possible that he may fall into the mistaken belief that because he has relieved himself of the duties and toils of the Long Path, he has little else to do than give himself up to idle dreaming and lazy optimism. No—he has taken on himself fresh duties and other toils, even though they are of a different kind. He has to learn the true meaning of "pray without ceasing" as well as to practise it. He has to meditate twenty times a day, even though each session will not be longer than a minute or two. He has to recollect himself, his essential divinity, a hundred times a day. All this calls for incessant work and determined effort, for the exercise of energy and zeal. (23-6-206)

The attitudes of reverence, even awe, devotion, worship, ought not to be eliminated just because he is practising the Short Path. It is still a technique even if it does embody the assumption of nonduality. (23-1-117)

Most Short Path teachings lack a cosmogony. They evade the fact that God is, and must be, present on the plane of manifestation and expressing through the entire universe. Why? (23-2-19)

The Short Path is, in essence, the ceaseless practice of remembering to stay in the Stillness, for this is what he really is in his innermost being and where he meets the World-Mind. (23-1-97)

God is in your very being. To know him as something apart or far-away in time and distance or as an object outside yourself, separate from you—that is not the Way—impossible. Jesus gave away the secret: he is within you. (25-1-50)

If the real Self must have been present and been witness to our peaceful enjoyment of deep slumber—otherwise we would not have known that we had had such enjoyment—so must it likewise have been present and been witness to our rambling imaginations in dream-filled sleep and to our physical activities in waking. This leads to a tremendous but inescapable conclusion. We are as near to, or as much in, the real Self, the Overself, at every moment of every day as we ever shall be. All we need is awareness of it.

(22-3-25)

To attach oneself to a guru, an avatar, one religion, one creed, is to see the stars only. To put one's faith in the Infinite Being and in its presence within the heart, is to see the vast empty sky itself. The stars will come and go, will disintegrate and vanish, but the sky remains. (28-2-104)

When all of a man's thoughts are put together, this total constitutes his ego. By giving them up to the Stillness, he gives up his ego, denies his self, in Jesus' phrase. (8-4-200)

A boundless faith in the Overself's power to assist him must be the possession of a Short Path votary—that is, faith in both the existence and the efficacy of its Grace. (23-1-121)

He must call in a new power, and a higher power—Grace. He needs its help. For the ego will not willingly give up its sovereignty, however much it may become preoccupied with spiritual questions and even spiritual growth. (23-4-59)

Not by his ego's own will can he take hold of this jewel, but only by the Grace substituting that other Consciousness for his ego's. (23-4-93)

It is the unique contribution of the Short Path that it takes advantage of the Overself's ever-present offer of Grace. (23-1-134)

It does not lie within man's power to gain more than a glimpse of this diviner life. If he is to be established firmly and lastingly in it, then a descent of grace is absolutely necessary. Artificial methods will never bring this about. Rites and sacrifices and magical performances, puzzling over Zen koans or poring over the newest books, will never bring it. (18-5-100)

The average spiritual aspirant is unduly self-centered. This is because he is so preoccupied with his own development, his own self-correction, and his own spiritual needs that he tends to forget a vitally important truth. This is that the last battle to be fought on the Quest—the battle which brings the ego finally and fully under the Overself's rule—is reflected to a lesser extent in the earlier battles of the Quest. This battle cannot possibly be won by the aspirant himself for the very good and sufficient reason that the ego is not willing to commit suicide, or to put it in another way, is unable to lift itself onto a plane of non-existence. Final victory can only come by the bestowal of Grace from the Overself, which alone can effect this seeming miracle. To attract this Grace the seeker needs to turn away from his self-centeredness to what is its utter opposite—preoccupation with the Overself. He is to think of the Divine alone, of the infinitude and eternity of the Higher Power, and to forget all about his personal growth for a while. (23-4-70)

The closer he comes to the Overself, the more actively is the Grace able to operate on him. The reason for this lies in the very nature of Grace, since it is nothing other than a benign force emanating from the Overself. It is always there but is prevented by the dominance of the animal nature and the ego from entering his awareness. When this dominance is sufficiently broken down, the

Grace comes into play more and more frequently, both through Glimpses and otherwise. (18-5-101)

When he shifts the centre of his interest from the ego to the Stillness his life begins to manage itself. Happenings pertaining to it come about without his doing anything at all. (23-1-150)

It is while working with the Short Path that the man discovers he may apply its principles to his worldly existence, his earthly fortunes too. He learns that the ultimate source of his physical welfare is not the ego but the Overself. If he looks only to the little ego for his supply, he must accept all its narrow limitations, its dependence on personal effort alone. But if he looks farther and recognizes his true source of welfare is with the Overself, with its miracle-working Grace, he knows that all things are possible to it. Hope, optimism, and high expectation make his life richer, more abundant. (23-1-146)

The Short Path makes miracles possible because it leads through the gate of the timeless, futureless, pastless Now. (23-1-164)

Aspiration which is not just a vague and occasional wish but a steady settled and intense longing for the Overself is a primary requirement. Such aspiration means the hunger for awareness of the Overself, the thirst for experience of the Overself, the call for union to the Overself. It is a veritable power which lifts one upward, which helps one give up the ego more quickly, and which attracts Grace. It will have these desirable effects in proportion to how intensely it is felt and how unmixed it is with other personal desires. (18-1-53)

If you are getting no result, no change in external situation, it is because you are not *practising*. You are dependent upon the feeble little ego. Cultivate the idea incessantly that the Overself *provides* and put yourself in dependence on its higher power. But do not attempt this before you have studied and appropriated the lessons of your existing circumstances. (23-4-169)

If he is willing to look for them, he will find the hidden workings of the ego in the most unsuspected corners, even in the very midst of his loftiest spiritual aspirations. The ego is unwilling to die and will even welcome this large attrition of its scope if that is its only way of escape from death. Since it is necessarily the active agent in these attempts at self-betterment, it will be in the best position to take care that they shall end as a seeming victory over itself but not an actual one. The latter can be achieved only by directly confronting it and, under Grace's inspiration, directly slaying it; this is quite different from confronting and slaying any of its widely varied expressions in weaknesses and faults. They are not at all the same. They are the branches but the ego is the root. Therefore when the aspirant gets tired of this never-ending Long Path battle with his lower nature, which can be conquered in one expression only to appear in a new one, gets weary of the self-deceptions in the much pleasanter imagined accomplishments of the Short Path, he will be ready to try the last and only resource. Here at long last he gets at the ego itself by completely surrendering it, instead of preoccupying himself with its numerous disguises—which may be ugly, as envy, or attractive, as virtue. (8-4-164)

Nature cannot be hastened. The bloom of a flower opens in its own proper time. If the Short Path yields immediate or quick results to some aspirants, it is only because they are persons of superior development. They have served their apprenticeship on the Long Path already, either in this life or previous lives. (23-4-9)

Think more deeply than the conventional mass of guru-followers dare to do and you will come to perceive that in the end there is only one Teacher for each man, his own Overself; that all other and outer gurus are merely channels which IT uses. "It is He who lives inside and speaks through the outer guru's voice," declares a Tibetan text. Why not go direct to the source? (1-6-821)

The Short Path man ought not to depend on authorities, scriptures, rules, regulations, organizations, gurus, or writings. His past history may outwardly force such an association on him, but inwardly he will seek to liberate himself from it. For his ultimate aim is to reach a point where no interpreter, medium, or transmitter obtrudes between him and the Overself. (23-1-83)

The Overself takes his thoughts about it, limited and remote though they are, and guides them closer and closer to its own high level. Such illumined thinking is not the same as ordinary thinking. Its qualitative height and mystical depth are immensely superior. But when his thoughts can go no farther, the Overself's Grace touches and silences them. In that moment he *knows*.

(4-4-18)

The Short Path offers a swifter unfoldment of the intuitional consciousness. It is not so bound to the limitation of time as the Long Path is. It seeks to identify the man *now* with his higher self. (23-5-76)

Why create needless frustrations by an overeager attitude, by overdoing spiritual activity? You are in the Overself's hands even now and if the fundamental aspiration is present, your development will go on without your having to be anxious about it. Let the burden go. Do not become a victim of too much suggestion got from reading too much spiritual literature creating an artificial conception of enlightenment, just as too much reading of medical literature by a layman may make him the victim of hypochondriac tendencies. Do not be satisfied with the self-conscious spirituality which comes from forced growth and harsh unnatural asceticisms, or from egocentrically watching personal progress. That is a better and truer spirituality which is natural, as natural as waking from sleep; which is unforced, because not the result of following technique and practising exercises; which is unconscious, growing and blooming as the flower does; which is drawn by the Overself's beauty and warmth and peace.

(23-5-232)

The period of active effort is at an end; the period of passive waiting now follows it. Without any act on his own part and without any mental movement of his own, the Grace draws him up to the next higher stage and miraculously puts him there where he has so long and so much desired to be. Mark well the absence of self-effort at this stage, how the whole task is taken out of his hands. (23-7-242)

In its advanced phases the Short Path is no pathway at all. It has all the freedom of air and sea. (23-1-110)

The Long Path

As a Preparation

He who enters upon this quest will have plenty to do, for he will have to work on the weaknesses in his character, to think impartially, to meditate regularly, and to aspire constantly. Above all, he will have to train himself in the discipline of surrendering the ego. *(Perspectives* 2-16)

If the Grace of the Overself is to take hold of the man, no part of his ego ought to offer resistance. This is why a preparation for the event is needed, a process of taking out of him those things which are certain to instigate such resistance. In other words, the activity of the Long Path is necessary to the successful treading of the Short Path. (23-4-21)

It would be wonderful if everyone, everywhere, could slip so easily into the kingdom of heaven, and just as easily stay there forever. But alas! the facts of human nature forbid it. People require teaching, training, purifying, disciplining, and preparing, before they can do so. And the course needed is a lifetime's, the work needed much and varied. That is why the Long Path is needed. (23-4-1)

The "purification" which he is to seek through the Long Path is not the narrow limited and intolerant kind which too often is called by this name. It is not at all merely a harsh denial of the sexual instinct. It is a cleansing of consciousness, of his thought-life, his emotional life, and even of his bodily condition. Its aim is to prepare his consciousness so that it can receive the truth without deflecting or warping or blocking it. Inevitably the most important work and always the most difficult work along this line will be the elimination of the ego's tyranny. (23-4-26)

Every negative thought and base desire is an obstacle to the attainment of the higher consciousness. This is why the Long Path's work is needed, for it is intended to remove all such obstacles. How can one invite that Consciousness to dwell in a body enslaved by lusts, or in a mind darkened by hates? (23-4-36)

To confess sins of conduct and shortcomings of character as a part of regular devotional practice possesses a psychological value quite apart from any other that may be claimed for it. It develops humility, exposes self-deceit, and increases self-knowledge. It decreases vanity every time it forces the penitent to face his faults. It opens a pathway first for the mercy and ultimately for the Grace of the higher Self. (18-3-72)

Although the possibility of this discovery and awareness of Overself and establishment in it has always been with every man at every moment, the probability has not. For he has to develop the equipment for maturing from animal *through* man's gathered experience to this full establishment in full union with his highest being. The savage may get the glimpse, and does, but this is only a beginning, not an end. The teaching favoured by Indian metaphysicians that we came from God and shall return to God is an oversimplification which generally leads to misunderstanding. Then all this long pilgrimage with all its sufferings becomes a senseless waste of time and an idiotic expenditure of energy—if not on our part then on God's. It is like banging one's head against a wall in order to enjoy the relief which follows when the action ends. Through lack of a cosmogony the proponents of this teaching are compelled to explain away the purpose of all this vast universe as non-purpose, using the term *maya*, one of whose two meanings is "mystery." The Infinite Being, whose Consciousness and Power is behind the universe of history, can itself have no history, for it is beyond time, evolution, change, development, can have no purpose which is gainful to itself, cannot be made the object of human thought correctly because it utterly transcends the limitations of such thought. But all this is not to say that the World-Mind's activity is meaningless, Idea-less, and fruitless. The very contrary is the case.   (26-4-258)

Students who have come finally to philosophy from the Indian *Advaita Vedanta*, bring with them the belief that the divine soul having somehow lost its consciousness is now seeking to become self-conscious again. They suppose that the ego originates and ends on the same level—divinity—and therefore the question is often asked why it should go forth on such a long and unnecessary journey. This question is a misconceived one. It is not the ego itself which ever was consciously divine, but its source, the Overself. The ego's divine character lies in its essential but hidden being, but it has never known that. The purpose of gathering experience (the evolutionary process) is precisely to bring it to such awareness. The ego comes to slow birth in finite consciousness out of utter unconsciousness and, later, to recognition and union with its infinite source. That source, whence it has emanated, remains untouched, unaffected, ever knowing and serenely witnessing. The purpose in this evolution is the ego's own advancement. When the Quest is reached, the Overself reveals its presence fitfully and brokenly at first but later the hide-and-seek game ends in loving union. (26-4-256)

Nearly everyone would most likely choose a way which evaded all the long discipline of thought and feeling, all the stern reform of bodily habits, and yet brought him swiftly to the goal and gave him in full its glorious rewards. This choice is pardonable and seemingly sensible. But observation and experience, study and research, show that such a way exists only in theory, not in factuality; that its dramatic successes are the rare cases of a very few geniuses; that those who take this seemingly easy and short road mostly arrive, if they arrive at all, at a state of intellectual intoxication and pseudo-illumination; and that where their reward for this Short Path practice is a genuine Glimpse, they wrongly believe it to be the End of the Road and cease all further effort to grow. (23-2-59)

Those who believe in the Short Path of sudden attainment, such as the following of Ramana Maharshi and the koan-puzzled intellectuals of Zen Buddhism, confuse the first flash of insight which unsettles everything so gloriously with the last flash which settles everything even more gloriously. The disciple who wants something for nothing, who hopes to get to the goal without being kept busy with arduous travels to the very end, will not get it. He has to move from one point of view to a higher, from many a struggle with weaknesses to their mastery. Then only, when he has done by himself what he should do, may he cease his efforts, be still, and await the influx of Grace. Then comes light and the second birth. (23-2-65)

That inspired and excellent little book, Brother Lawrence's *The Practice of the Presence of God,* is an example of Short Path teaching. The contemporary biographer of Lawrence writes: "He could never regulate his devotion by certain methods as some do. . . . At first, he had meditated for some time, but afterwards that went off." "All bodily mortifications and other exercises are useless," he thought, "but as they serve to arrive at the union with God by love." Now it is all very well for Brother Lawrence to decry techniques and to tell aspirants that his prayer or method was simply a sense of the presence of God. He himself needed nothing more than to attend to what was already present to, and existing in, him. But how many average aspirants are so fortunate, how many possess such a ready-made sense or feeling? Is it not the general experience that this is a result of long previous toil and sacrifice, an effect and not itself a cause? (23-2-68)

Many fixations created in the past have to be removed before we can truly live in the present. This is Long Path work. (23-4-16)

Until he enters the Short Path it cannot be said that Grace is more than partially possible. Until he has lifted himself by his own endeavours to some extent above the animality with which he struggles on the Long Path and into the calmness which is necessary to the practice of the Short one, he has hardly earned the reward of Grace in its fullness or frequency. (23-4-38)

Because the Overself is already there within him in all its immutable sublimity, man has not to develop it or perfect it. He has only to develop and perfect his ego until it becomes like a polished mirror, held up to and reflecting the sacred attributes of the Overself, and showing openly forth the divine qualities which had hitherto lain hidden behind itself. (1-5-12)

The man who is devoid of the eight qualities which practice of the Long Path eventually develops in him will not be able to succeed in practising the Short Path. These qualities are calmness, self-control, oriental withdrawal, fortitude, faith, constant recollection, intense yearning for the Overself, and keen discrimination between the transient and the eternal. (2-5-49)

Unless he loves the Overself with deep feeling and real devotion, he is unlikely to put forth the efforts needed to find it and the disciplines needed to push aside the obstacles in the way to it.

(18-1-92)

What or who is seeking enlightenment? It cannot be the higher Self, for that is itself of the nature of Light. There then only remains the ego! This ego, the object of so many denunciations and denigrations, is the being that, transformed, will win truth and find Reality even though it must surrender itself utterly in the end as the price to be paid. (8-4-435)

Another reason for the need of the Long Path's preparatory work is that the mind, nerves, emotions, and body of the man shall be gradually made capable of sustaining the influx of the Solar Force, or Spirit-Energy. (23-4-35)

As a Limitation

There are certain patterns of thought which reflect the idea that attainment of this goal is almost impossible, and that the needed preparation and purification could not be even half finished in a whole lifetime. If these patterns are held over a long period of years, they provide him with powerful suggestions of limitation.

Thus the very instruction or teaching which is supposed to help his progress actually handicaps it and emotionally obstructs it. His belief that character must be improved, weaknesses must be corrected, and the ego must be fought looms so large in his outlook that it obliterates the equally necessary truth that Grace is ever at hand and that he should seek to invoke it by certain practices and attitudes. (23-2-109)

The man on the Long Path reaches a point where he tends to overdo its requirements or to do them in an unbalanced way. He is then too self-conscious, too much ridden by guilt, oscillating between indulgence and remorse. Only when his efforts seem to be futile and his mind to be baffled, only when he gives up in exhaustion does he give up the tension which causes it. Then, relaxed, spontaneity released, the gate is at last open for grace to enter. In its light he may see that in one sense he had been running around in circles because he had been running around inside his own ego. (23-4-135)

The Long Path, despite its magnificent ideals of self-improvement and self-control, is still egoistic. For this determination to rise spiritually is directed by willed ambition—willed by the higher part of the ego. (23-2-105)

The processes and procedures of the Long Path require time. But the Overself is outside of time. To identify yourself with them is to shut yourself out from it. It is consequently needful when a certain point is reached—either in experience or in preparation or in understanding—to abandon the Long Path and take to the Short Path, with its emphasis on living in the Eternal Now. (23-4-144)

He stands athwart the door and blocks it from opening to the gentle pressure of the very Grace which can bring him the help for which he calls out. Less preoccupation with his own ego and more with the Overself is what he really needs. This is the same as saying that the Long Path work now needs balancing with Short Path work. (23-4-52)

The aspirant who frequently measures how far he has advanced, or retrograded, upon this path, or how long he has stood still, is seeking something to be gained for himself, is looking all the time at himself. He is measuring the ego instead of trying to transcend it altogether. He is clinging to self, instead of obeying Jesus' injunction to deny it. Looking at the ego, he unwittingly stands with his back to the Overself. If he is ever to become enlightened, he must turn round, cease this endless self-mea-surement, stop fussing over little steps forward or backward, let all thoughts about his own backwardness or greatness cease, and look directly at the goal itself. (2-2-45)

The Long Path keeps the mind continually searching, whether for increased holiness or increased truth. It is never quiet, content, at peace. (23-2-114)

Although the ego claims to be engaged in a war against itself, we may be certain that it has no intention of allowing a real victory to be achieved but only a pseudo-victory. The simple conscious mind is no match for such cunning. This is one reason why out of so many spiritual seekers, so few really attain union with the Overself, why self-deceived masters soon get a following whereas the true ones are left in peace, untroubled by such eagerness. (8-4-316)

The way of the Long Path is an effort to abstract him from the bonds of physical appetite and passion which prevent his free thought and balanced feeling. It is an effort of disentanglement. But by its very nature this is only a negative attainment. It must be followed by a positive one. And the latter must enable the man to fulfil life's higher purpose in the midst of human worldly activity, while yet enabling him to keep the freedom he has won through self-discipline. Therein lies the superiority of the Short Path.   (23-4-40)

The attempt to liberate self by self must prove in the end to be a vicious circle, an experiment in futility. The Unconditioned cannot be brought by finite man into his grasp. It must come of Itself and bring him within Its Grace. Yet unless the attempt is made, unless the Long Path is travelled, the aspirant is little likely to be sufficiently equipped to succeed with the Short Path.   (23-4-17)

He comes in the end to recognize his ineffectiveness and incapacity, to admit that he cannot rightly hope to succeed on the quest by his own efforts or by his own qualities. This may make him unhappy but it also offers the opportunity to make himself truly humble.   (23-4-118)

At first he learns that he is personally responsible for his thoughts and actions, for their results in himself and outside it in his destiny. Then if he accepts this truth and in the Long Path works upon it, he is led to the discovery of the Short Path and that he is God's responsibility.   (23-4-42)

Because it is impossible for the questing ego to become the Overself, the quester must recognize that he is the Overself and stop thinking in egoistic terms of progress along a path, or attainment of a goal. (22-3-26)

The path of dealing with his shortcomings one by one is not only too long, too slow, but also incomplete and negative. It is concerned with what not to be and not to do. This is good, but it is not enough. It pertains to the little ego. He must add to it the path of remembering his higher all-self. This is a positive thing. More, it brings the Grace which finishes the work he has already started. It carries him from the ego's past into the Overself's Eternal New. (23-5-173)

The humility needed must be immensely deeper than what ordinarily passes for it. He must begin with the axiom that the ego is ceaselessly deceiving him, misleading him, ruling him. He must be prepared to find its sway just as powerful amid his spiritual interests as his worldly ones. He must realize that he has been going from illusion to illusion even when he seemed to progress. (18-3.20)

The end of all his efforts on the Long Path will be the discovery that although the ego can be refined, thinned, and disciplined, it will still remain highly rarefied and extremely subtle. The disciplining of the self can go on and on and on. There will be no end to it. For the ego will always be able to find ways to keep the aspirant busy in self-improvement, thus blinding him to the fact that the self is still there behind all his improvements. For why should the ego kill itself? Yet the enlightenment which is the goal he strives to reach can never be obtained unless the ego ceases to bar the way to it. At this discovery he will have no alternative to, and will be quite ready for, the Short Path. (23-4-119)

Moving from the Long
to the Short Path

THE TIME will come when you will have to turn your back upon the Long Path in order to give full attention, the full energy and the full time, to the Short Path. For with this comes a new era when the whole concern is not with the ego, not with its improvement or betterment, but with the divine itself alone—not with the surface consciousness and all its little changes but with the very depths, the diviner depths where reality abides. At this point seek only the Higher Self, live only with positive thought, stay only for as long as you can with the holy silence within, feel only that inner stillness which belongs to the essence of consciousness. Henceforth you are not to become this or that, not to gather the various virtues, but simply to be. For this you do not have to strive, you do not have to think, you do not have to work with any form of yoga, with any method of meditation.   (23-1-76)

When body and feeling are cleansed by disciplinary regimes, when the intellect is inspired by meditational exercises, one is ready for the Short Path.   (23-1-135)

When he has reached this stage he will begin to understand that his further spiritual progress does not impose special acts such as disciplinary regimes and meditation exercises—excellent and necessary though these were in their place as preparatory work

—but requires him simply to stand aside and be an observing witness of life, including his own life. (23-4-140)

The Long Path is taught to beginners and others in the earlier and middle stages of the quest. This is because they are ready for the idea of self-improvement and not for the higher one of the unreality of the self. So the latter is taught on the Short Path, where attention is turned away from the little self and from the idea of perfecting it, to the essence, the real being. (23-4-6)

If he keeps on fixing his attention upon fighting the wandering characteristic of his thoughts, he may find after many attempts that the task seems impossible. Why is this? It is because at the same time he is limiting himself to attention upon the ego. Let him move in the opposite direction and turn to the Short Path, let the thoughts fix themselves on the Overself, upon Its great stillness, Its serene impersonality. The ego will not and cannot remove itself by itself but by going outside to THAT which is its origin. The thoughts in the end are led into surrender to the power which transcends it and will master it. (23-4-72)

They are too self-conscious about their work and progress on this quest, their adoption of it and experiences in it. It is only when they leave this Long Path for the Short one that their attitude becomes spontaneous, unstudied, natural, their feelings released from ambition, affectation, and egocentricity. They begin to "grow as the flower grows," as Mabel Collins puts it. (23-4-75)

There are two different approaches to the task; both are legitimate, but one belongs to the Long Path and the other to the Short Path. The first is forcibly to control the undesirable feelings and thoughts. The second is to seek their source in the ego and, by understanding it at this deep level, lose interest in them and, turning away, stop continuing to feed them. (23-4-74)

The way to the goal does not lie through a cleansing of the ego alone: it lies also through a desertion of it. The first way is necessary only because it helps to make the second one possible. (23-4-19)

If he could stop being in love with his ego and start being in love with his Overself, his progress would be rapid. (8-4-157)

On the Long Path we analyse the past and study the present so as to learn the basic lessons of the ego's experience. On the Short Path we discard analysis and dispense with study; instead we contemplate the God in us. If the first path brings us unhappy reflections, the second one brings joyous intuitions. (23-5-101)

Although the two Paths are so sharply divided from one another in theory, they not seldom overlap in fact. (23-5-32)

All the more elementary and religious and occult forms of meditation, including those used on the Long Path—all that lead to what the Hindu yogis call *savikalpa samadhi*—usually have to be passed through; but one ought not to remain with them. The pure philosophic meditation as ultimately sought and reached on the Short Path is to put the attention directly on the Overself and on nothing else. (23-5-104)

If you investigate the matter deeply enough and widely enough, you will find that happiness eludes nearly all men despite the fact that they are forever seeking it. The fortunate and successful few are those who have stopped seeking with the ego alone and allow the search to be directed inwardly by the higher self. They alone can find a happiness unblemished by defects or deficiencies, a Supreme Good which is not a further source of pain and sorrow but an endless source of satisfaction and peace.   (24-1-74)

It is an error to believe that men can separate themselves permanently from normal human life, and themselves exist as if they were ghosts. They may succeed in doing so for a time, a period, sometimes even a lifetime, but in the end the bipolar forces which control development will draw them back. No such separation is desired or sought on the Short Path—as it often is on the Long one—and those who follow it can appreciate physical or cultural possessions and satisfactions. But because they are spiritually mature, there is always inner detachment behind this appreciation.   (23-5-57)

It is certainly better to remove faults and remedy weaknesses than to leave them as they are. But it is not enough to improve, refine, ennoble, and even spiritualize the ego. For all such activity takes place under the illusion that the ego possesses reality. This illusion needs to be eliminated, not merely changed for another one.

(23-2-119)

To become their ruler you may fight desires. This is the harder way. Or you may forget them. This is the easier way. To follow it you must practise remembering the Overself constantly. (23-4-100)

The virtues he attempted to acquire on the Long Path, and too often attempted in vain, come to him of themselves by the magical grace of the Short Path.   (23-1-161)

In this way he does little to free himself from a weakness, a desire, or a passion. It goes, falls away of its own accord, if he looks to the Higher Self rather than to the management of his own ego for salvation. It is in this spontaneous way, too, that the attitude of detachment begins to appear in his character and little by little —but sometimes swiftly—becomes established. But a warning is needed here. Whatever purifications or strengthenings, whatever other attempts and trainings at self-betterment he has begun need not be dropped, provided they are kept in their place and not allowed to obscure the view of the primary goal or gradually sidetrack direction from its superior level. (23-1-168)

If the Long Path creates despair about oneself, about the frustration of one's spiritual hopes, the Short Path creates joy about one's close relationship with the Overself and the feeling of its acceptance of one. (23-5-111)

It is only on the Long Path that a man seeks so desperately for truth and insight. All that feverish ambition fades away on the Short Path, where he learns to hold himself in peace and patience. (23-5-96)

Pessimism can only appear on the Long Path, for it must disappear on the Short Path. Here the emphasis is on positive values; the declarations are affirmative ones. The Short Path inculcates joyousness and advocates contentment. (23-5-79)

It is the personal ego which operates the will and tries to bring about the result. This is quite proper and pertinent on the Long Path practice. But when attention is turned away from it to the Short Path, it is no longer the will but the higher power which should be looked to for the result. (23-5-113)

If the Long Path begins and ends with ego, the Short Path begins with a 180 degree turnaround, opens up a vista of the infinite Overself. (23-1-35)

If the Long Path equips him with the necessary strength, purity, and concentration, the Short Path makes use of this equipment to unite his consciousness directly with the Overself. (23-4-11)

If the Long Path seeks salvation chiefly through the building of character and the concentration of thought, the Short Path seeks it chiefly through worshipful meditation directly on the Overself. (23-5-19)

On the Long Path his actions follow, or try—however badly—to follow, the rules. They are imitative actions. But on the Short Path he becomes an individual, living from the inside out. (23-5-93)

On the Long Path the man is preoccupied with techniques to be practised and disciplines to be undergone. On the Short Path he is preoccupied with the Overself, with the study of its meaning, the remembrance of its presence, and the reflection upon its nature and attributes. (23-5-6)

The Long Path votary works from systems, rules, plans, and techniques put down by its guides but the Short Path votary has no path chalked out for him. He is forever "waiting on the Lord." (23-5-72)

The Long Path brings the self to a growing awareness of its own strength, whereas the Short Path brings it to a growing awareness of its own unreality. This higher stage leads inevitably to a turnabout face, where the energies are directed toward identification with the One Infinite Mind. The more this is done, the more Grace flows by reaction into the Self.   (23-5-61)

What is grace? It is a descent of the Overself into the underself's zone of awareness. It is a visitation of power as unexpected and unpredictable as it is welcome and gratifying. It is an unseen hand stretched forth from the world-darkness amid which we grope with unsteady feet. It is the voice of the Overself speaking suddenly out of the cosmic silence with which we are environed. It is like a glorious rainbow of hope which suddenly appears when all seems lost.

More precisely, grace is a mystical energy, an active principle pertaining to the Overself which can produce results in the fields of human thought, feeling, and flesh alike on the one hand, or in human karma, circumstances, and relations on the other hand. It is the cosmic will, not merely a pious wish or kindly thought, and can perform authentic miracles under its own unknown laws. Such is its dynamic potency that it can confer insight into ultimate reality as easily as it can lift a dying person back to life again or instantaneously restore the use of limbs to a crippled one.

(Wisdom of the Overself, p. 207)

It has been said that the Short Path is absolutely necessary because the ego on the Long Path cannot by all its own efforts attain enlightenment. The higher individuality must come into play, and that entry onto the scene is called grace. This does not mean an arbitrary intervention, favouring one person and repulsing another. It comes by itself when the proper conditions have been prepared for it, by the opening or surrender of the self, by the turning of the whole being to its source. This openness, surrender, or passivity to the Other is not to be attained by quietening the thoughts alone. The mind is open then but it has to be opened to the highest, directed to the highest, aspiring to the highest. Otherwise, there is the mere passivity of the medium, or of the thought-reader, without the divine presence. (18-5-201)

The same Grace which starts us off on the Quest carries us through to its end. The Short Path phase begins when we awaken to the presence of the Grace's source. (23-4-80)

On the Long Path we search for truth, reality, the Overself. That is, we use the ego's forces and faculties. On the Short one we keep still and let truth, reality, the Overself's Grace search for us instead. The ego is then no longer in the picture. (23-5-78)

The work of the Long Path is to loathe and remove the ego's sins; that of the Short Path is to love and receive the Overself's grace. (23-5-114)

The Long Path calls for a continued effort of the will, the Short one for a continued loving attention. (23-5-88)

The Long Path is splattered with discouragements. Only those who have sought to change themselves, to remold their characters, to deny their weaknesses, know what it is to weep in dissatisfaction over their failures. This is why the Short Path of God-remembrance is also needed. For with this second path to fulfil and complete the first one, Grace may enter into the battle at any moment and with it victory will suddenly end the struggles of many years, forgiveness will suddenly wipe out their mistakes.

(23-5-170)

The man who enters the Long Path is too often seeking compensation for disappointment, whereas the man who enters the Short one usually is attracted to the joy of fulfilment in the Overself.

(23-5-83)

The Long Path developed in him through yoga-meditation the capacity to find the inner Stillness. The Short Path added to it (1) the knowledge that the Stillness is himself, and (2) the practice of continuing remembrance to *be* the Stillness. (23-4-8)

The Long Path is arranged in progressive stages, whereas the Short Path is not; it points to direct, immediate, and final enlightenment. (23-5-98)

The Long Path is devoted to clearing away the obstructions in man's nature and to attacking the errors in his character. The Short Path is devoted to affirmatives, to the God-power as essence and in manifestation. It is mystical. It shows how the individual can come into harmonious relation with the Overself and the World-Idea. The first path shows seekers how to think rightly; the second gives power to those thoughts. (23-5-1)

The Long Path practitioner looks upon illumination as something to be attained in the future when all requirements have been fully met, whereas the Short Path devotee looks upon it as attainable here and now. (23-5-90)

The Long Path is more easily practised while engaged in the world, the Short Path while in retreat from it. The experiences which the vicissitudes of worldly life bring him also develop him, provided he is a Quester. But the lofty themes of his meditations on the Short Path require solitary places and unhurried leisurely periods.   (23-5-65)

The Long Path sets up an attitude of yearning whereas the Short Path considers the Spirit an ever-present fact and consequently there is no need to yearn for it!   (23-5-89)

The Long Path wants to purify and perfect the ego but the Short Path wants to find God. The Long Path deals with the little pieces of a design but the Short Path deals with the pattern itself. The Long Path takes one minor theme after another but the Short one takes up the main underlying theme alone. It is also the difference, as well as distance, between the immediate goal and the ultimate one.   (23-5-40)

The Long Path follower, with his strenuous concern for self-improvement, his compelling anxiety for self-advancement to fulfil the inner purposes of life, may make life more difficult than it need be and himself become more humourless. The Short Path follower can afford to forget his past struggles, and begin to enjoy life.   (23-5-63)

The Long way is also called the Earth Path. The Short way is also called the Sun Path. This is because the earth is subject to gloomy seasonal changes but the sun never varies in its radiance. If the Long Path is somewhat austere, the Short one is notably joyous.   (23-5-73)

The Short Path depends on naturalness and spontaneity—quite the opposite of the Long Path's discipline and effort. The individual who turns aside from the latter at the right moment does so not because he spurns them or denies them or rejects them but because they do not serve him now. (23-4-133)

On the Short Path he becomes aware of the fact of forgiveness. He leaves out the constant self-criticism and self-belittling, the painstaking self-improvement practices, of the other Path and begins to take full note of this saving fact. (23-5-29)

While the Long Path man is busy worrying about the evil in himself and in the world, the Short Path man is busy smiling at the good in the Overself and in the World-Idea. (23-5-33)

There is no wish in the Short Path man to be better than he is, no desire to improve his character or purify his mind, no sense of being obliged to rectify the distortions brought about by the ego in both thought and feeling. (23-5-86)

Wu Wei has a double meaning: first, letting Life, Mind, act through you by yourself, becoming still, thought-free, and empty of ego— you are then not doing anything, but being done to, being used; second, pursuing truth impersonally. The usual ways seek personal attainment, achievement, salvation. The aspirant thinks or speaks of "my mind" or "my purification" or "my progress"; hence such ways are self-enclosed, egoistic. Whatever repression of ego that there is occurs only on the surface and merely drives it down to hide in the subconscious, whence it will re-emerge later. These methods are Long Path ones, hence are destined to end in futility and despair. The deeper way of Wu Wei is to lose the ego by doing nothing to seek truth or to improve oneself; adopting no practice; following no path. The Short Path turns realization over to Overself so that it is not your concern any longer. This does not mean that you do not care whether you find truth or not, but that whereas ordinary care for it arises out of desire of the ego or anxiety of the ego or egoistic need of comfort, escape, or relief, Short Path care arises out of the stillness of mind, the serenity of faith, and the acceptance of the universe.   (23-5-228)

4

Awareness: "Who Am I?"

Why is it that so many people are so unaware of their own higher existence? The answer is that their faculty of awareness itself is that spiritual existence. Whatever they know, people know through the consciousness within them. That in them which knows anything is their divine element. The power of knowing—whether it be a thought that is known, a complex of thoughts such as memories, a thing such as a landscape—is a divine power for it derives from the higher self which they possess.   (21-5-48)

It is a quest to become conscious of Consciousness, to explore the "I" and penetrate the mystery of its knowing power.   (1-1-20)

If we want certain knowledge, instead of vague hope, that the answer to this question "Who am I?" is "I am of godlike essence," we must follow the Quest into its disciplines and practices.   (2-1-5)

The mysterious question "Who Am I?" is certainly deeply important, which is why it was put forward from the very beginning of his career by Ramana Maharshi. There is also another question which one may venture to state: "Where Am I?" Am I here in the fleshly body or in the invisible mind?   (21-5-140)

Everything remembered is a thought in consciousness. This not only applies to objects, events, and places. It also applies to persons, including oneself, he who is remembered, the "I" that I was.

This means that my own personality, what I call myself, was a thought in the past, however strong and however persistent. But the past was once the present. Therefore I am not less a thought now. The question arises what did I have then which I still have now, unchanged, exactly the same. It cannot be "I" as the person, for that is different in some way each time. It is, and can only be, "I" as Consciousness. (8-2-3)

The knowledge that no two human beings are alike refers to their bodies and minds. But this leaves out the part of their nature which is spiritual, which is found and experienced in deep meditation. In that, the deepest part of their conscious being, the personal self vanishes; only consciousness-in-itself, thought-free, world-free, remains. This is the source of the "I" feeling, and it is exactly alike in the experience of all other human beings. This is the part which never dies, "where God and man may mingle." (22-3-380)

The presence is always there, always waiting to be recognized and felt, but inner silence is needed to make this possible. And few persons possess it or seek it. (24-4-52)

That we know this awareness exists means only that we have an *idea* of awareness. We do not see that awareness as itself an object, nor can we ever do so. If we are to know the awareness by itself, first we would have to drop knowing its objects, its reflections in thought, including the ego-thought, and then be it, not see it. (21-5-168)

If we search into the innermost part of our self, we come in the end to an utter void where nothing from the outside world can reflect itself, to a divine stillness where no image and no form

can be active. This is the essence of our being. This is the true
Spirit.   (23-7-149)

In the Void the Real is hidden, all time is rolled up there: the
entire world and the space holding it dissolves there, everything
and everyone emerges and vanishes there. THAT alone is the
ever-Real, ever-Being. That is what man must learn to consider
as his own hidden being, a task of re-identification.   (19-5-17)

In that silent centre there is immense power and rocklike
strength.   (24-4-107)

The Overself perceives and knows the individual self, but only
as an imperturbable witness—in the same way that the sun witnesses the various objects upon the earth but does not enter
into a particular relation with a particular object. So too the
Overself is present in each individual self as the witness and as
the unchanging consciousness which gives consciousness to the
individual.   (22-3-338)

There is only a single light of consciousness in the mind's camera.
Without it the world could not be photographed upon the film
of our ego-mind. Without it, the ego-mind itself would be just as
blank. That light is the Overself.   (8-1-78)

When man shall discover the hidden power within himself which
enables him to be conscious and to think, he will discover the holy
spirit, the ray of Infinite Mind lighting his little finite mind.

                                                              (22-3-181)

Consciousness appearing as the person seeks itself. This is its quest. But when it learns and comprehends that it is itself the object of that quest, the person stops not only seeking outside himself but even engaging in the quest itself. Henceforth he lets himself be moved by the Overself's flow. (23-1-3)

Too often beginners regard lofty emotions or extraordinary powers or ecstatic rapture as the measure of attainment, when the only genuine measure is "awareness." (25-2-25)

Everything else can be known, as things and ideas are known, as something apart or possessed, but the Overself cannot be truly known in this way. Only by identifying oneself with It can this happen. (22-3-190)

This is the spiritual climax of one's life, this dramatic moment when consciousness comes to recognize and understand itself.
(25-2-247)

5

The Ego & The Overself: "What Am I?"

What we commonly think of as constituting the "I" is an idea which changes from year to year. This is the personal "I." But what we feel most intimately as being always present in all these different ideas of the "I," that is, the sense of being, of existence, never changes at all. It is this which is our true enduring "I."

(8-2-1)

Think! What does the "I" stand for? This single and simple letter is filled with unutterable mystery. For apart from the infinite void in which it is born and to which it must return, it has no meaning. The Eternal is its hidden core and content.   (8-1-8)

There is some life-power from which we derive our capacities and our intelligence. It is hidden and intangible. No one has seen it but everyone who thinks deeply enough can sense that it is there, always present and always supporting us. It is the Overself.

(22-3-175)

The true self of man is hidden in a central core of stillness, a central vacuum of silence. This core, this vacuum occupies only a pinpoint in dimension. All around it there is a ring of thoughts and desires constituting the imagined self, the ego. This ring is constantly fermenting with fresh thoughts, constantly changing with fresh desires, and alternately bubbling with joy or heaving with grief. Whereas the centre is forever at rest, the ring around it is never at rest; whereas the centre bestows peace, the ring destroys it. (8-1-32)

Our attachment to the ego is natural. It arises because we are unconsciously attached to that which is behind it, to the Overself. Only, we are misled by ignorance wholly to concentrate on the apparent "I" and wholly to ignore the unseen, enduring self of which it is but a transient shadow. The "I" which trembles or enjoys in the time-series is not the real "I." (8-2-18)

The personal ego has its singularities and particularities, its present aims and past memories, its life within time, its own temperament and special characteristics. All this amounts to this: it is unique. The individuality is the highest, subtlest, and finest, even divinest part of being. It is out of time. It is pure essence, the other is a compounded entity. For it the hours do not pass; for the other there is a constant sequence, a moment-to-moment existence. Sometimes men catch a glimpse of it, this other self which is really their own best self and which is not something to be attained by a progression since it is forever present. It does not have or need thoughts. Every moment which they give to identifying themselves with it is their salvation. If this takes one far from kith and kin, from all speech with all persons, it also carries him into a diviner relationship and communication with them. (8-1-143)

There is no real ego but only a quick succession of thoughts which constitutes the "I" process. There is no separate entity forming the personal consciousness but only a series of impressions, ideas, images revolving round a common centre. The latter is completely empty; the feeling of something being there derives from a totally different plane—that of the Overself. (8-2-31)

What is the ego but the Overself surrounded with barriers, conditioned by its instruments—the body, the feelings, and the intellect—and forgetful of its own nature? (8-1-6)

Each person is stuck in his own ego until the idea of liberation dawns on him and he sets to work on himself and eventually grace manifests and puts him on the Short Path. (8-5-415)

That a theme for meditation should be formulated in the interrogative is at once an indication that the kind of meditation involved is intellectual. *What am I?* is a simple question with a complex answer.

In this exercise you will repeatedly think of what you really are as distinct from what you seem to be. You will separate yourself intellectually, emotionally, and volitionally—so far as you can—from your flesh, your desires, and your thoughts as being objects of your consciousness and not pure consciousness itself. You will begin by asking yourself "Who am I?" and, when you comprehend that the lower nature cannot be the real you, go on to asking the further question: "What am I?" By such frequent self-studies and self-discriminations, you will come closer and closer to the truth. (4-4-36)

The Overself is not merely a transient intellectual abstraction but rather an eternal presence. For those who have awakened to the consciousness of this presence, there is always available its mysterious power and sublime inspiration. (22-2-69)

The Overself does not evolve and does not progress. These are activities which belong to time and space. It is nowhere in time and nowhere in space. It *is* Here, in this deep beautiful and all-pervading calm, that a man finds his real identity. (22-3-245)

This beneficent, freedom-bestowing, character-transforming, soul-awakening, gentle Presence is Overself. (22-3-253)

When in deep sleep we have absolutely no sense of Time's existence at all. We are then in eternity! When we become thoroughly convinced of the illusoriness of time, and make this conviction a settled attitude, eternity reveals itself even during the waking state. This is life in the Overself. This is not the same as totalizing the past present and future; all those belong to illusion. This realization gives perfect peace. (19-4-84)

Although the Overself does not pass through the diverse experiences of its imperfect image, the ego, nevertheless it witnesses them. Although it is aware of the pain and pleasure experienced by the body which it is animating, it does not itself feel them; although detached from physical sensations, it is not ignorant of them. On the other hand, the personal consciousness does feel them because it regards them as states of its own self. Thus the Overself is conscious of our joys and sorrows without itself sharing them. It is aware of our sense-experience without itself being physically sentient. Those who wonder how this is possible should reflect that a man awakened from a nightmare is aware once again in the form of a revived memory of what he suffered and what he sensed but yet does not share again either the suffering or the sensations. (22-3-337)

If a man could withdraw sufficiently from his ego to stop letting its interests and desires overpower him, he would thereby let peace come to triumph in his heart. The true paradise, the real heavenly kingdom, which has been postponed by an ignorant clergy to the post-mortem world, thus becoming far-off and elusive, is in fact as near to us as our own selves, and as present as today. If we are to enter it, we can and must enter while yet in the flesh. It is not a time or place but a state of life and a stage of development. It is the ego-free life. The ego is not asked to destroy itself but to discipline itself. The personal in a man must live, but only as a slave to the impersonal. These two identities make up his self.

(8-1-208)

Resurrection—to die and live again—is a symbol. It means to leave the ego and enter the Overself *in full consciousness*.   (20-5-7)

This identification with the best Self in us is the ideal set for all men, to be realized through long experience and much suffering or through accepting instruction, following revelation, unfolding intuition, practising meditation, and living wisely. And this best Self is not the most virtuous part of our character—though it may be one of the sources of that virtue—but the deepest part of our being, underneath the thoughts which buzz like bees and the emotions which express our egotism. A sublime stillness reigns in it. There in that stillness, is our truest identity.   (1-5-18)

The mysterious character of the Overself inevitably puzzles the intellect. We may appreciate it better if we accept the paradoxical fact that it unites a duality and that therefore there are two ways of thinking of it, both correct. There is the divine being which is entirely above all temporal concerns, absolute and universal, and there is also the demi-divine being which is in historical relation with the human ego.   (22-3-386)

This is the paradox, that the Overself is at once universal and individual. It is the first because it overshadows all men as a single power. It is the second because it is found by each man within himself. It is both space and the point in space. It is infinite Spirit and yet it is also the holy presence in everyone's heart.   (22-3-384)

Why I chose *"What Am I"*: (1) Because I wanted to start with the idea of a non-"I" consciousness instead of their own "I" with which they are continuously occupied; (2) Because the word *Brahman* is of neuter gender, neither masculine nor feminine. Brahman in us is *Atman,* the Self—but utterly impersonal. "What" lends itself more easily to this impersonality than "Who"; (3) The answer to *"What Am I?"* is multiple but it begins with "a part of the world!" and is followed by another question, "What is my relation to this world?" The answer requires the discovery of Mentalism, leading back through the thought of the world, thinker, and consciousness, to Brahman.   (8-1-36)

The answer to the question *"What am I?"* is "A divine Soul." This soul is related to, and rooted in, God. But that does not make us equivalent to God. Those who say so are using language carelessly.   (8-1-38)

The inability of little man to enter into the knowledge of transcendent God does not doom him to perpetual ignorance. For God, being present in all things, is present in him too. The flame is still in the spark. Here is his hope and chance. Just as he knows his own personal identity, so God knows God in him as the Overself. This divine knowing *is continually going on, whether he is awake or asleep, whether he is an atheist or a saint.* He can share in it too, but only by consenting to submit his intellect to his intuition. This is not an arbitrary condition imposed by theocratic whim but one which inheres in the very nature of the knowing processes. By accepting it, he may put the whole matter to the test and learn for himself, in due time, his other nonpersonal identity.   (28-2-89)

Man does not exist alone, isolate. He is himself part of the universe into which he is born. Therefore he cannot obtain an adequate answer to the question "What am I?" unless he also obtains an answer to the question "What is my relationship to the universe?" Consequently the mystic who is satisfied with the answer which he discovers through meditation to the first question, is satisfied with a half-truth. (16-2-251)

Perceive these two things now: the dreamlike character of life in the world, and the illusory character of the personal ego. Hence the need of the "What am I?" enquiry, that the illusion of the ego may be dispelled. When you can see these things clearly, then you may be still and undisturbed, unentangled, and unillusioned amid the struggle of life. You will be wise, free, impervious to the petty persecution of men—their lies, malice, and injuries—for being no longer identified with the personality, you are no longer their target. (21-5-4)

The source of wisdom and power, of love and beauty, is within ourselves, but not within our egos. It is within our consciousness. Indeed, its presence provides us with a conscious contrast which enables us to speak of the ego as if it were something different and apart: it is the true Self whereas the ego is only an illusion of the mind. (8-1-2)

Is it possible to unite both ways, the active life in the world outside and the quiet life in the stillness within, and find no break, no essential difference, no falsification of the oft-stated idea, "God is everywhere"? The answer is Yes! and has been tested in ancient and modern experience. "What is the World?" gives the same reply as "Who am I?" Withdrawing from the physical sense-world as the mystic does or going into physical action with the senses engaged need not break the union, the awareness of divine presence. (20-4-104)

The ego self is the creature born out of man's own doing and thinking, slowly changing and growing. The Overself is the image of God, perfect, finished, and changeless. What he has to do, if he is to fulfil himself, is to let the one shine through the other.

(8-1-7)

How close is his relationship to that other Self, that godlike Overself! And not only his mind's relationship but also his body's. For in the centre of every cell in blood, marrow, flesh, and bone, there is the void that holds, and is, pure Spirit.   (5-2-36)

The ego is not really killed—how without body and intellect, emotion and will, could anyone act in this world?—but the centre of being is moved out of it to the Overself.   (P-8-20)

Once this question—*what am I?*—is answered, there are no other questions. In the light of its dazzling answer, he knows how to handle all his problems.   (8-1-11)

Mentalism: The Key to Non-Duality

Mentalism, the teaching that this is a mental universe, is too hard to believe for the ordinary man yet too hard to disbelieve for the illumined man. This is because to the first it is only a theory, but to the second it is a personal experience. The ordinary man's consciousness is kept captive by his senses, each of which reports a world of matter outside him. The illumined man's consciousness is free to be itself, to report its own reality and to reveal the senses and their world to be mere ideation.

(21-4-45)

It is all like a gigantic dream, with every human inserting his own private dream inside the public one. A double spell has to be broken before reality can be glimpsed—the spell which the world lays upon us and that which self lays upon us. The man who has completely awakened from this spell is the man who has gained complete insight. This faculty is nothing other than such full wakefulness. It is immensely difficult to attain, which is why so few of the dreamers ever wake up at all and why so many will not even listen to the revelations of the awakened ones. However, Nature teaches us here as elsewhere not to let patience break down. There is plenty of time in her bag. Life is an evolutionary process. Men will begin to stir in their sleep erratically but increasingly.   (20-4-194)

While the dream is still continuing, he cannot help taking its scenes and figures as being quite real. But if someone rings a bell until he awakens from the dreaming state, he will then see that both scenes and figures were mere figments of his own imagination. In a sense, the teacher of philosophy acts as this awakener did, except that he directs his efforts to the sense-deceived consciousness of everyday life. (1-6-28)

Krishna, in the *Bhagavad Gita,* is the individual's own higher self. He must keep his inner shrine within the heart reserved for the Ideal. He should worship there the Spirit that is birthless and deathless, indestructible and divine. Life in this world is like foam on the sea: it passes all too soon; but the moments given in adoration and obeisance to the Soul count for eternal gain. The most tremendous historic happenings on this earth are, after all, only pictures that pass through consciousness like a dream. Once the seeker awakens to the Real, he sees them for what they are. Then he will live in Its serenity, and it will no longer matter if the pictures themselves are stormy and agitated. It is the greatest good fortune to attain such serenity—to be lifted above passion and hatred, prejudice and fear, greed and discontent, and yet to be able to attend effectively and capably to one's worldly duties. It is possible to reach this state. The seeker may have had glimpses of it already. Someday, sometime, if he is patient, he will enter it to stay—and the unimaginably rewarding and perfect purpose of his life, of all his lifetimes, will be fulfilled. (18-1-5)

The illuminate sees objects as other persons do, only his sense of materiality is destroyed, for he sees them too as *ideas*, unreal. The illuminate's viewpoint is *not* the yogi's viewpoint. The illuminate finds all the world in himself, says the *Gita.* This means he feels sympathetically at one with all creatures, even mosquitoes or snakes. (21-5-24)

The two analyses must come together now, simultaneously: the "What Am I?" and the "What is the World?" Then only can they be unified by mentalism, reappearing in, and as, the One Consciousness; the duality of self and non-self vanishes. (21-5-155)

It is not the five senses which know the world outside, since they are only instruments which the mind uses. It is not even the intellect, since that merely reproduces the image formed out of the total sense reports. They are not capable of functioning by themselves. It is the principle of Consciousness which is behind both, and for which they are simply agents, that really makes awareness of the world at all possible. It is like the sun, which lights up the existence of all things. (21-1-56)

Not only is the world an appearance-in-Consciousness, but so is the ego. It is in the end a thought, perhaps the strongest of all; and only the Consciousness-in-Itself is the Reality from which it draws sustenance, existence, life. (21-5-138)

The teaching of nonduality is that *all* things are within one and the same element—Consciousness. Hence there are no two or three or three million things and entities: there is in reality only the One Consciousness. (28-1-26)

If the investigation of time made in depth by intelligence shows the real essence of it to be an eternal Now, so a similar investigation of space shows its real essence to be an eternal Here. Both these results are also to be reached in actual experience sharply and clearly in meditation in depth. But where are they?

The answer is given briefly and precisely by mentalism: they are in consciousness. (19-4-53)

Earth life is but a dream, lived out in a dream physical body amid dream environment. Dream experiences are only ideas; during sleep-dream man sees, hears, touches, tastes, and smells exactly as he does during waking-dream. Hence waking is but materialized ideas, but still *ideas*. God's cosmic dream: all universal activities are but different ideas of God, divine ideation made material and thrown upon the screen of human consciousness. The cosmic illusion is impinged upon man's sense and seen from within by Mind through consciousness, sensation, and bodily organ.

(21-3-23)

The *Vedantin* tells you, "Your experience of the world is illusory; you take it to be existent; you see a snake when there is only a rope." But the philosopher comments: "It is misleading only if while you are in the body you take it to be utterly and ultimately real. The world is actually there, but what is it that makes it there for you? Consciousness! *That* is the reality. But what you call consciousness is only a fragment, a very small confined thing, compared with its source." (21-5-176)

In the waking state we experience the physical world, in the dream state our experience corresponds to the etheric astral world, in the deep sleep state we enter a still higher level of experience which is that of the God whose will is expressed in the other and lower two worlds. This God the Hindus call *Ishvara*; I have called it World-Mind. Now underlying these three states and therefore the Reality, the consciousness, the real consciousness underneath them, man experiences as enlightenment. The other three are states whereas this is the Reality supporting those three states—waking, dream, and deep sleep. In deep sleep man reaches God, it might be said, but owing to his ignorance he is unaware so he does not benefit by it. (19-3-193)

Consciousness really does exist whereas the things which it makes known are present only when they are perceived, felt, heard, or otherwise sensed by one or more of the five reporting agents. This consciousness is in itself always the same, unvarying, the one thing in us in which thoughts and bodies make their appearance and from which they also vanish. (21-1-80)

Inwardly and daily he returns to this idea that all is Idea, that the familiar world—its places and people, its city life seething with activity, its vaunted civilization and polished culture—has no other existence than in his consciousness and takes its reality from that. So to become conscious of Consciousness detached from its productions—thoughts—is his task, draws his strength and devotion. (21-5-16)

The mental images which make up the universe of our experience repeat themselves innumerable times in a single minute. They give an impression of continuity and permanency and stability only because of this, in the same way that a cinema picture does. If we could efface them and yet keep our consciousness undiminished, we would know for the first time their source, the reality behind their appearances. That is, we would know Mind-in-itself. Such effacement is effected by yoga. Here then is the importance of the connection between mentalism and mysticism. (21-5-206)

The student has to stand aside from the thought-forms, which means that he must stand aside from the person and look at it as something external to himself. If and when he succeeds in getting behind it, he automatically adopts the standpoint of the Overself. He must make the person an object and the Overself its observer. Now this element of pure awareness is something constant and unbroken; hence it is not ordinary consciousness, which is a discontinuous thing made of totalized thoughts, but transcendental consciousness. (23-6-83)

The world looks just as it did before; being understood for what it is—a thought-series—does not alter its appearance. The sage's perception of it is like other men's; his senses function like theirs; but he knows that his experience of it depends on the ever-presence of Consciousness; *he is never without this awareness.* This is the large first difference. (21-5-142)

(a) "The one without a second" reappears in the universe as "no two things alike." (b) Nonduality, not two, means mentalism; the world is my idea, in my consciousness, hence not separate from me. There are not two—me plus world. (19-2-18)

Reality is to be found neither by thinking alone nor by not thinking at all. This high path which opens to the philosophic student is one of unwavering deeply abstract concentration of the mind in the real, whether the mind be thinking or not thinking, and whether the individual be acting or not acting. (20-4-99)

The understanding that everything is illusive is not the final one. It is an essential stage but only a stage. Ultimately you will understand that the form and separateness of a thing are illusory, but the thing-in-itself is not. *That* out of which these forms appear is not different from them, hence Reality is one and the same in all things. This is the paradox of life and a sharp mind is needed to perceive it. However, to bring beginners out of their earthly attachments, we have to teach first the illusoriness of the world, and then raise them to a higher level of understanding and show that the world is not apart from the Real. *That Thou Art* unifies everything in essence. But this final realization cannot be got by stilling the mind, only by awakening it into full vigour again after yogic peace has been attained and then letting its activity cease of its own accord when thought merges voluntarily into insight. When that is done, you know the limitations of both yoga and enquiry as successive stages. Whoever realizes this truth does not divorce from matter—as most yogis do—but realizes non-difference from it. Hence we call this highest path the "yoga of nonduality." But to reach it one has to pass through the "yoga of philosophical knowledge."

(25-2-116)

There are two viewpoints: a qualified truth for the lower stage of aspirants which admits duality; and the complete viewpoint of nonduality for the highest student; thus for practical life, when dealing with other people or when engaged in some activity, those in the first stage must accept the notion of the world being real, because of expediency; yet even so, when they are alone or when keeping quiet, inactive, they ought to revert back to regarding the world, which includes one's own body as a part of it, as idea. Only for the sage is the truth always present, no matter whether he is with others, whether he is working, or whether he is in trance, and this truth is continuous awareness of one Reality alone and one Self alone. (19-2-40)

There is only one mind and all such names as cosmic mind, over-mind, and so forth are merely imperfect and partial concepts of that ultimate single mind which philosophy puts forth in order to help students advance to a higher stage. These concepts are not false, however. They represent aspects of the same ultimate mind as seen from different standpoints. As these standpoints are not the highest they do not yield the final truth. It will be well therefore for him to accustom himself to the highest standpoint and to remember always that there is but one mind, one reality, one principle, one substance, one being only. All things are forms or shapes which it appears to take temporarily. The key to the understanding of these admittedly difficult points is to think of the universe seen during dream and then to remember that that universe itself, its seas and continents, its peoples and animals, its happenings in time, its distances in space, do not exist apart from the mind of the dreaming person; that even if millions of people exist within that universe they are nothing else than ideas passing through the mind of the dreamer; and that their ultimate stuff or reality is mind although to the dreamer they appear real, as do also water, fire, gas, and even the ninety-odd chemical elements. Now he must try to regard the waking universe in the same way, with this difference: that because the ego is one of the dreamed-of figures in the waking dreams it must be eliminated if one is to break through the dream and ascertain that it is a dream in the universal mind.   (21-3-44)

The term nonduality remains a sound in the air when heard, a visual image when read. Without the key of mentalism it remains just that. How many Vedanta students and, be it said, teachers interpret it aright? And that is to understand there are no two sep-arate entities—a thing and also the thought of it. The thing is in mind, is a projection of mind as the thought. This is nonduality, for mind is not apart from what comes from and goes back into it. As with things, so with bodies and worlds. All appear along with the ultimately cosmic but immediately individual thought of them.   (28-1-25)

To arrive at the understanding that the universe is non-material and is mental, is to be liberated from materialism. It produces a sensation like that felt by a prisoner who has spent half a life-time cooped up in a dark and dingy fetid dungeon and who is suddenly liberated, set free, put out of doors in the bright sunshine and fresh clean air. For to be a materialist means to be one imprisoned in the false belief that the matter-world is the real world; to become spiritual is to perceive that all objects are mental ones; the revelation of the mental nature of the universe is so stupendous that it actually sets mind and feeling free from their materialistic prison and brings the whole inner being into the dazzling sunshine of truth, the fresh atmosphere of Reality. All those who believe in the materiality of the material world and not in its mental nature, are really materialists—even if they call themselves religious, Christians, spiritualists, occultists, or Anthroposophists. The only way to escape materialism is not to become a follower of any psychic cult or religious faith, but to enquire with the mind into the truth of matter and to be rewarded at length by the abiding perception of its mental Nature. All other methods are futile, or at best are but preparatory and preliminary steps.   (21-5-96)

It is a fundamental error to turn the pure mind into an object of experience in an attempt to reach comprehension. Mind can know everything else and is the inescapable condition of every experience, for by its light every object and every event is revealed, but it cannot itself be known in the same way that we know every-thing else. Ordinarily there is a knower and a known, and mind would have to transcend such a relation were it to become aware of itself, which means that it would have to transcend thinking itself. Mind itself produces the categories of time, space, and cause which make world experience possible and knowable—that is, thinkable—which is why it cannot be grasped in the same way. The nature of mind is unique, and before its sublime verity speech trembles into silence. (28-2-74)

We must move from consciousness to its hidden reality, the mind-essence which is alone true consciousness because it shines by its own and not by a borrowed light. When we cease to consider Mind as this or that particular mind but as all-Mind; when we cease to consider Thought as this thought or that but as the common power which makes thinking possible; and when we cease to consider this or that idea as such but as pure Idea, we apprehend the absolute existence through profound insight. Insight, at this stage, has no particular object to be conscious of. In this sense it is a Void. When the personal mind is stripped of its memories and anticipations, when all sense-impressions and thoughts entirely drop away from it, then it enters the realm of empty unnameable Nothingness. It is really a kind of self-contemplation. But this self is not finite and individual, it is cosmic and infinite. (23-8-8)

When we understand this truth (mentalism), we shall understand that the Overself is forever present with us and that this presence is more immediate and intimate than anything else in life.

(21-5-125)

Warnings on the Short Path

THE ADVOCATES of the Short Path teach that with its entry, all necessity for the toils processes and disciplines of the Long one ceases. They are right. But they are rarely right when it comes to applying this statement to individual cases. For then it is nearly always applied prematurely. The results are then disastrous at most, disappointing at least.   (23-4-149)

Most beginners are not usually ready for the entire Short Path. They ought not attempt more than its simpler practices, such as those concerned with recollection of the Quest and remembrance of the Overself. If they attempt the more advanced exercises, such as self-identification with the Overself or cultivation of the attitude which rejects evil's reality, they are likely to put themselves in a false, self-deceived position. That is, the attempt to ignore the ego does not eradicate it but merely alters its pattern. If it seems to be absent because the divine is present, the transformation has taken place in imagination, not in actuality. It would be better to postpone the advanced part until they have done enough preparatory work on the Long Path, and thus cleansed their emotions, developed mental controls, and balanced their temperament.   (23-2-3)

The Long Path is unutterably irksome whereas the Short Path is gloriously attractive. The one is associated with toil and suffering; its emblem is the Cross. The other is associated with peace and joy; its emblem is the Sun. Yet, those who would prematurely desert the one for the other will find their hopes frustrated in the end, however enthusiastic and rapturous the experience may be in the beginning. This is because Nature, the Overself, will not let them enjoy permanently what must be taken into every part of their being, properly cleansed and prepared to absorb it, with the being itself properly equilibrated to endure the experience of absorption without stimulating the ego. (23-2-1)

Those who are ill-qualified for the Short Path, who come to it in order to escape the tiresome disciplines of the Long Path, who want a sudden and swift enlightenment without having to pass through the gradations of slowly preparing themselves for it, usually find themselves thrown back in the end. (23-2-99)

There are certain other dangers to which enthusiasts for the various Short Paths are exposed. They read books devoted to descriptions of the attainments and goals and become captivated by what they read and charmed by what they are taught. Then they begin to imitate what they can and to imagine what they cannot. In the end they fall into ego-centered fantasies and ego-fostered deceptions. They think they are more exalted in attainment than they really are. But so subtle is this disguised spiritual egoism that they are quite unaware of their peril until disaster deflates it. (23-2-47)

The danger of becoming too self-centered exists on the Long Path but the danger of deifying the self exists on the Short one.

(23-5-34)

If he begins with the Short Path he may feel that whatever is accomplished is self-accomplished and thus, subtly, insidiously, his ego will triumphantly reassert, or keep, its supremacy. But if he begins with the Long Path and, after all his efforts, reaches an inconclusive result, the consequent despair may crush his ego and point up his dependence on, and need of, Grace.   (23-5-103)

The introduction of the Short Path ought not to be mistimed; it ought not to be introduced until enough work has been done to prepare a moral and intellectual basis for it, and enough balance secured. Then only will its capacity to lead the seeker toward the glorious climax of his quest be actualized. If introduced too early it merely stimulates egotism, animates intellectual pride, or simulates illumination.   (23-2-2)

The attempt to ignore order of development in the Quest, to leap from the lowest to the highest stages, to miss all the intervening ones, is an attempt to get something for nothing. It cannot succeed. For the influx of Spirit needs a chalice clean enough to be fit for it, large enough to hold it. What would happen if the influx were poured into a dirty, cracked, tiny, and weak vessel?

(23-4-33)

The dangers inherent in the Short Path have to be noted and even proclaimed. The self-identification with the divine leads to the idea that since it is sinless the practiser is sinless, too, and whatever he does is right. Such an idea can come only to those who unconsciously seek excuses to justify the satisfaction of their desires. To them, the Long Path with its exhortations to self-control and self-discipline is something to be evaded. Another danger is the conceited belief that since the divine is ever-present, the goal has been attained and nothing further need be done— no exercises, no study, no meditation, and of course no ascetic regimes. It is such dangers which were part of the reasons why, in former times, the hidden teaching was not communicated to any persons until their character was first secretly and carefully tested for maturity and their mind was tested for fitness. This caution was as existent in Christian circles as in Hindu ones. Today, since it has largely been broken down, the results are to be seen in the West as well as in the East, among solitary obscure individuals as well as among publicized cults. They are to be seen in mental derangement and immoral licence, in parrot-like prattle and charlatanic deception. (23-2-7)

Those who are impatient with the restraints, the labours, and the disciplines of the Long Path may take prematurely to the Short Path. The result, as seen in the cases of younger people, is unhealthy. They get intoxicated with their new freedom and may take unrestrictedly to drink, drugs, sex, and general slovenliness of speech, manner, and dress. The absence of the idea of sin from their outlook may produce an irresponsibility dangerous to themselves and disturbing to society. (23-2-36)

The Short Path schools are correct in asserting that if we gain the Overself we shall also gain the purity of heart and goodness of character which go with it. But they omit to point out that such a gain will be quite temporary if we are unable to remain in the Overself. (23-2-53)

Without this conquest of the lower nature no enlightenment can remain either a lasting or an unmixed one. And without suitable disciplines, no such conquest is possible. This is one reason why it is not enough to travel the Short Path. (23-5-171)

The claim that if the true self is found, all the qualities and attributes which pertain to it will also be found, naturally and automatically, at the same time is a valid one. How could the qualities and attributes of the lower nature thrive or even exist in that rarefied air? They would instantly be displaced by the higher ones. But what is overlooked by, or unknown to, the makers of this claim, is that the period of such displacement would, and could, only be a temporary one. "Nature never leaps toward what she will eventually bring about," Goethe announces, and truly. As soon as the impetus which launched him into the deep waters of the Spirit exhausts itself, as it must if he is still unpurified, unprepared, and undeveloped, the man will be thrown back to the place where he belongs. His illumination will not have enough basis to be securely established and so will turn out to be only a passing glimpse. (23-2-41)

Holding on to this awareness of the Overself automatically brings with it control over the body's appetites and desires. This is one of the benefits of success on the Short Path, but such easy spontaneous control lasts no longer than the awareness. (23-2-9)

There is no need to think twice to understand that this is a dangerous doctrine. If a man believes that he is already divine and has nothing more to gain in that way, pitfalls lie ahead of him: first, self-deception leading to spiritual arrogance; second, indolence leading to lack of any effort to purify character and better the mind. The end could be a smug dwelling in illusion, very far from the divine reality it is supposed to be. Out of such illusions step forth the ambitious leaders of little groups or large movements, claiming special knowledge, power, vision, authority, even messiahship. (23-2-4)

The Short Path devotee who believes he has nothing to do and can leave all to the master, or to the Overself, believes wrongly. Such spiritual idleness may lull him pleasantly into a thin contentment but this is not the same as real inner peace won by grappling in the right attitude with difficulties as they come, or by keeping the personal will submissive during tests and obedient during temptations. (23-2-46)

It is understandable that aspirants would like to save themselves from the exertions demanded by the Long Path, and would prefer to receive sufficient Grace to grant them the desired higher experiences. But if they turn the existence of the Short Path into an excuse to avoid these exertions, they are unlikely to gain what they want. (23-2-31)

Beware of losing balance in the study of metaphysical truth or in the practice of the Short Path, of imagining that you are surpassing the intellect and getting spiritually illumined. Beware of getting intellectually drunk with your own self-importance and emotionally intoxicated with your own self-glorification. Such study can be very stimulating. Beware of coming to believe that you have found the Divine in a single flash, overnight. Have you really become God? Is omnipotence really yours? (23-2-39)

He has not attained who is conscious that he has attained, for this very consciousness cunningly hides the ego and delivers him into its power. That alone is attainment which is natural, spontaneous, unforced, unaware, and unadvertised, whether to the man himself or to others. (25-2-85)

It is a fallacy to think that this displacement of the lower self brings about its complete substitution by the infinite and absolute Deity. This fallacy is an ancient and common one in mystical circles and leads to fantastic declarations of self-deification. If the lower self is displaced, it is not destroyed. It lives on but in strict subordination to the higher one, the Overself, the divine soul of man; and it is this latter, not the divine world-principle, which is the true displacing element. (25-2-198)

They consider themselves to be free from the possibility of committing sin, since they are joined to the divine consciousness. They do not regard the moral codes of society as binding upon them, since they are a law unto themselves. Whatever they do, it can only be right. The dangers here are, of course, first, that the ego's desire may only too easily be mistaken for the divine ordinance, and second, that all things are permitted to them. Since they feel that they are in a state of grace, there is no longer any controlling power to judge, criticize, or curb their acts, no outside help to warn them when they go perilously astray. (23-2-20)

The Short Path leads to a continual happiness, for it refuses to look upon the world's sorrows and one's own troubles but cheerfully gazes beyond them toward the eternal and impersonal blessedness. But since it can do this theoretically only, for realization depends on Grace, the happiness may one day vanish when fact collides with faith. (23-2-16)

Because good and bad have no meaning on the plane where there is no opposition, no struggle between them, the "enlightened" man who taught others to ignore this opposition and abandon this struggle, who told them that to do what they will is the whole of the law, would thereby prove his own lack of enlightenment. In other words, he would be a dangerous impostor or a mere intellectual. (23-2-17)

It is a matter that comes to the careful observer's attention that in groups or societies, in ashrams or institutions, where what is practised corresponds to the Short Path—however roughly and imperfectly—the results are very mixed and often saddening to the leaders. Where no attempt is made to bring in the Long Path's corrective work, where there is no striving for self-improvement, the end is a confused one—some satisfactions but more disappointments. (23-5-149)

The Philosophic Solution: Balance the Paths

The advocates of the Long Path claim that the mind must be trained and the heart must be cleansed before enlightenment is possible. The advocates of the Short Path claim that it is sufficient to deny the ego and affirm the higher self. The philosopher studies the facts revealed by observation and research and concludes that the methods of both schools must be united if enlightenment is not only to be lastingly attained but also not to fall short of its perfect state. (23-5-166)

The twofold way is indispensable: on the one hand the way of self-effort, working to overcome the ego, and on the other the way of Grace, through constantly seeking to remember your true identity in the Overself. (23-5-193)

How can a person fully express himself unless he fully develops himself? The spiritual evolution which requires us to abandon the ego runs parallel to the mental evolution which requires us to perfect it. (8-1-158)

The Quest uses the whole of one's being, and when enlightenment comes, all parts are illumined by it. To prepare for this, one should continue the self-humbling prayers for Grace, the exercise of sudden remembrance of the Overself, the surrender of the lower nature to the Higher, and the never-ceasing yearning for Reality. (2-5-70)

If we think, "I strive to become one with God," or, "I am one with God," we have unconsciously denied the statement itself because we have unconsciously set up and retained two things, the "I" and "God." If these two ultimately exist as separate things they will always exist as such. If, however, they really enter into union, then they must always have been in union and never apart. In that case, the quest of the underself for the Overself is unnecessary. How can these two opposed situations be resolved? The answer is that relativity has taught us the need of a double standpoint, the one relative and practical and constantly shifting, the other absolute and philosophical and forever unchanged. From the first standpoint we see the necessity and must obey the urge of undertaking this quest in all its practical details and successive stages. From the second one, however, we see that all existence, inclusive of our own and whether we are aware of it or not, dwells in a timeless, motionless Now, a changeless, actionless Here, a thing-less, egoless Void. The first bids us work and work hard at self-development in meditation, metaphysics, and altruistic activity, but the second informs us that nothing we do or abstain from doing can raise us to a region where we already are and forever shall be in any case. And because we are what we are, because we are Sphinxes with angelic heads and animal bodies, we are forced to hold both these standpoints side by side. If we wish to think truthfully and not merely half-truthfully, we must make both these extremes meet one another. That is, neither may be asserted alone and neither may be denied alone. It is easier to experience this quality than to understand it.

This is puzzling indeed and can never be easy, but then, were life simple and less paradoxical than it is, all its major problems would not have worried the wisest men from the remotest antiquity until today. Such is the paradox of life and we had better accept it. That is, we must not hold one standpoint to the detriment of the other. These two views need not oppose themselves against each other but can exist in a state of reconciliation and harmony when their mutual necessity is understood. We have to remember both that which is ever-becoming and that which is ever in being. We are already as eternal, as immortal, as divine as we ever shall be. But if we want to become aware of it, why then we must climb down to the lower standpoint and pursue the quest in travail and limitation. (19-2-5)

The Vedantins, Zen Buddhists, Christian Scientists, and even to a certain extent Ramana Maharshi and Sri Krishna Menon said that self-identification with the Reality, thinking of this identification constantly, would be enough to attain the spiritual goal. This is called the Short Path. The opposite schools of Patanjali's Yoga, the Roman Stoics, and the Southern Buddhists reject this claim and say that it is necessary to thin down the ego and purify the mind by degrees through disciplines, exercises, and practices. This is called the Long Path. The Philosophic Method is to combine both of these schools of thought synthetically, with the explanation that both are necessary to complete each through the other—and that it depends upon the stage where the aspirant is as to which school is necessary for him or her to emphasize personally. Beginners need to give more weight to the hard effort of the Yoga school; but advanced persons need to give it to the Vedanta viewpoint, because in their case much of the ego-thinning and mental-emotional cleansing has already been done. (23-5-150)

Those who depend solely on the Short Path without being totally ready for it take too much for granted and make too much of a demand. This is arrogance. Instead of opening the door, such an attitude can only close it tighter. Those who depend solely on the Long Path take too much on their shoulders and burden themselves with a purificatory work which not even an entire lifetime can bring to an end. This is futility. It causes them to evolve at a slower rate. The wiser and philosophic procedure is to couple together the work on both paths in a regularly alternating rhythm, so that during the course of a year two totally different kinds of results begin to appear in the character and the behaviour, in the consciousness and the understanding. After all, we see this cycle everywhere in Nature, and in every other activity she compels us to conform to it. We see the alternation of sleep with waking, work with rest, and day with night. (23-5-159)

Ramana Maharshi was quite right. Pruning the ego of some faults will only be followed by the appearance and growth of new faults! Of what use is it so long as the ego remains alive? Hence the failure of mankind's moral history to show any real progress over the past three thousand years, despite the work of Buddha, Jesus, and other Messiahs. The correct course, which has always been valid for the individual, is just as valid for all mankind—get at the root, the source, the ego itself. But although Maharshi was right, his teaching gives only part of Truth's picture. Presented by itself, and without the other part, it is not only incomplete but may even become misleading. By itself it seems to indicate that there is no need to work on our specific weaknesses, that they can be left untouched while we concentrate on the essential thing—rooting out the ego. But where are the seekers who can straightaway and successfully root it out? For the very strength of purpose and power of concentration needed for this uprooting will be sapped by their faults. (23-5-183)

When the Overself is present in a man's consciousness, it is present in all his thoughts and actions. They are then under Its rule, they proceed from It. The man does not have to *seek* for any particular virtues, for all can and will then come of themselves as needed. Only then is any virtue solidly established. But until this presence is permanently secured, it would be foolish to cease working upon oneself, correcting oneself, improving oneself. A merely intellectual and theoretical acquaintance with this doctrine is inadequate. It is necessary until then to practise a coexistence of Short and Long Paths. (23-5-155)

It is quite true, as the extremist advocates of the Short Path, like Zen, say, that this is all that is really needed, that no meditation (in the ordinary sense), no discipline, no moral striving, and no study are required to gain enlightenment. We are now as divine as we ever shall be. There is nothing to be added to us; no evolution or development of our real self is possible. But what these advocates overlook is that, in the absence of the labours listed, the Short Path can succeed only if certain essential conditions are available. First, a teaching master must be found. It will not be enough to find an illumined man. We will feel peace and uplift in his presence, but these will fade away after leaving his presence. Such a man will be a phenomenon to admire and an inspiration to remember, not a guide to instruct, to warn, and to lead from step to step. Second, we must be able to live continuously with the teaching master until we have finished the course and reached the goal. Few aspirants have the freedom to fulfil the second condition, for circumstances are hard to control, and fewer still have the good fortune to fulfil the first one, for a competent, willing, and suitably circumstanced teaching master is a rarity. These are two of the reasons why philosophy asserts that a combination of both the Long and Short Paths is the only practical means for a modern Western aspirant to adopt. If, lured by the promise of sudden attainment or easy travelling, he neglects the Long Path, the passage of time will bring him to self-deception or frustration or disappointment or moral decline. For his negative characteristics will rise and overpower him, the lack of preparation and development will prevent him from realizing in experience the high-level teachings he is trying to make his own, while the impossibility of balancing himself under such circumstances will upset or rob him of whatever gains he may still make.   (23-5-151)

Practices for the Short Path

To practise the Short Path is to be aware of the miracle entailed in every moment of living. (23-1-115)

The Short Path is content with exercises done for their own sake, not for the sake of the results they bring. In this it is the opposite of the Long Path, which does them for results, and is attached to those results. (23-5-59)

There are three progressive stages in this technique. First, the student proves to *himself*, by following the master's guidance, that the ego is fictitious and illusory. Second, he concentrates diligently on Short Path meditation techniques to dig beneath the ego and escape from it. Third, he proves to himself the fact of Nonduality, that there is only the One Mind's existence. (23-6-1)

Different terms can be used to label this unique attainment. It is insight, awakening, enlightenment. It is Being, Truth, Consciousness. It is Discrimination between the Seer and the Seen. It is awareness of That Which Is. It is the Practice of the Presence of God. It is the Discovery of Timelessness. All these words tell us something but they all fall short and do not tell us enough. In fact they are only hints for farther they cannot go: it is not on their level at all since it is the Touch of the Untouchable. But never mind; just play with such ideas if you care to. Ruminate and move among them. Put your heart as well as head into the game. Who knows one day what may happen? Perhaps if you become still enough you too may *know*—as the Bible suggests.

(1-5-172)

The last phase of the Short Path has no special procedure, no specialized method. Life is its Way, or, as the Chinese sage said, "Usual life is very Tao." (23-5-226)

Love and Devotion

Jesus bade his hearers forsake their ego-selves if they would find the Overself. But *how* is a man to forsake that which he has loved so long, so intimately, and so ardently. What, in definite and precise details, is he to do? (8-4-199)

The feeling of being isolated, the sense of walking a lonely path, is true outwardly but untrue inwardly. For there he is companioned by the Overself's gentle ever-drawing love. He has only to grope within sufficiently to know this for himself, and to know it with absolute certitude. (1-3-321)

The way to be admitted to the Overself's presence can be summed up in a single phrase: *love it*. Not by breathing in very hard nor by blowing out very slow, not by standing on the head nor by contorting like a frog can admission be gained. Not even by long study of things divine nor by acute analysis of them. But let the love come first, let it inspire the breathing, blowing, standing, or contorting, let it draw to the study and drive to the thinking, and then these methods will become really fruitful. (18-1-78)

Love will have to enter his quest at some point—love for the Overself. For it is through this uniting force that his transformation will at the end be effected. (18-1-91)

His personal duty is to grow spiritually all he can as quickly as possible. He must concentrate on himself, but always keep at the back of his mind the idea that one day he will be fit to serve others and do something for them too. Spiritual growth entails meditation practices kept up as regularly as possible, metaphysical study, cultivation of intuition, and a kindling of an ever increasing love for the divine soul, the true "I." It is this soul which is the ray of God reflected in him and it is as near to God as anyone can ever get. God is too great, too infinite, ever to be completely comprehended; but the Overself, which is God's representative here, can be comprehended. Only it keeps itself back until he yearns for it as ardently as the most love-sick young man ever yearned for his sweetheart. It wants him to want it for its own sake, and because he has seen through all the material values and understands how imperfect they are in comparison. So he must cultivate this heartfelt love towards what is his innermost "me" and must not hesitate to pray for its Grace or even to weep for it. He must surrender inwardly and secretly all the ego's desires to it. (2-5-61)

Why purification of character should be needed in order to contact what seems to be above our lowly human characteristics is, indeed, a paradox which only the Overself can answer. Perhaps it is a test of our devotion—for it is known that the Higher Self will not surrender her revelations to anyone who does not love her completely. Purification is merely the casting out of lesser loves for the sake of this supreme Love. (6-1-160)

If there is any law connected with grace, it is that as we give love to the Overself so do we get grace from it. But that love must be so intense, so great, that we willingly sacrifice time and thought to it in a measure which shows how much it means to us. In short, we must give more in order to receive more. And love is the best thing we can give. (18-5-209)

If few attain the wonder of Overself consciousness, it is because few can lift their minds to the level of impersonality and anonymity. But what all cannot do with their minds, they can do much more easily with their hearts. Let them approach enveloped in love, and the grace will come forward to meet them. By its power, the ego which they could not bring themselves to renounce will be forgotten. (22-5-32)

Why does not the Overself show its existence and display its power once and for all? Why does it let this long torment of man, left to dwell in ignorance and darkness, go on? All that the ego is to gain from undergoing its varied evolution is wrapped up in the answer. This we have considered in *The Wisdom of the Overself* and *The Spiritual Crisis of Man*. But there is something more to be added to that answer. The Overself waits with deepest patience for him—man—to prefer it completely to everything and everyone else. It waits for the time when longings for the soul will leave the true aspirant no rest, when love for the divine will outlast and outweigh all other loves. When he feels that he needs it more than he needs anything else in this world, the Overself will unfailingly reveal its presence to him. Therefore a yearning devotion is one of the most important qualifications he can possess. (18-1-76)

First, he has a vague feeling of being attracted towards the Overself. Then he bestows more attention upon it, thinks of it frequently; at length attention grows into concentration and this, in turn, culminates in absorption. In the end, he can say, with al Hallaj: "I live not in myself, only in Thee. Last night I loved. This morning I am Love." (1-5-329)

Although he should give his best to external life, he should not give the whole of himself to it. Somewhere within his heart he must keep a certain reserve, a spiritual independence. It is here, in this secret place, that the supreme value of the Overself is to be cherished, loved, and surrendered to. (24-3-149)

The love which he is to bring as sacrificial offering to the Overself must take precedence of all other loves. It must penetrate the heart's core to a depth where the best of them fails to reach.

(18-1-82)

The personal attraction to, and affection for, the man Jesus can be usefully made into a focus for meditation. To meditate on the character, example, and teaching of one's spiritual Guide has long been a standard path in mysticism. It culminates in a joyous spiritual union, at which time the student becomes aware that the living presence of his chosen Guide is no longer separate from himself—his Real Self. This is what Jesus meant when he said, "I and My Father are One." It is, indeed, one of the shortest paths to the Goal. (4-5-123)

Love of the Overself is the swiftest horse that can bear us to the heavenly destination. For the more we love It, the less we love the ego and its ways. (18-1-93)

The more love he can bring into this practice, the more he is likely to succeed with it. If he cannot yet feel any love for the Overself, then let him bring joy into it, the joy of knowing that he is on the most worthwhile journey in life.   (4-2-296)

Who Am I?

The question "Who am I?" is asked somewhere in that monumental ancient book *The Yoga Vasistha*. It was often included centuries later by Saint Francis in his prayers. But Sri Ramana Maharshi gave it central importance in his advice to spiritual seekers and meditators.   (23-6-106)

There is something in each man which says "I." Is it the body? Usually he thinks so. But if he could set up a deeper analysis, he would find that consciousness would carry him away from the body-thought into itself. There, in its own pure existence, he would find the answer to his question, "Who am I?"   (8-1-67)

Follow the "I" back to its holy source.   (23-7-220)

If he will try to perceive the mind by which he perceives the world, he will be practising the shortest, most direct technique of discovering the Overself. This is what Ramana Maharshi meant when he taught, "Trace the 'I' to its source."   (22-5-6)

The ordinary kind of meditation seeks to escape from intellectualism at the very beginning, whereas the metaphysical kind uses it from the beginning. Even though it is analytic, it does not limit itself to cerebral activity; it conjoins feeling also, since it seeks an experience as well as understanding. Therefore, in the

"Who Am I?" work it moves with the whole being and with all its intensity. (4-4-62)

When you begin to seek the Knower, who is within you, and to sever yourself from the seen, which is both without and within you, you begin to pass from illusion to reality. (22-5-15)

Discover the Stillness

He will understand the real spirit of meditation when he understands that he has to do nothing at all, just to sit still physically, mentally, and emotionally. For the moment he attempts to do anything, he intrudes his ego. By sitting inwardly and outwardly still, he surrenders egoistic action and thereby implies that he is willing to surrender his little self to his Overself. He shows that he is willing to step aside and let himself be worked upon, acted through, and guided by a higher power. (23-7-238)

To the extent that a man keeps inwardly still, to that extent he unfolds himself and lets the ever-perfect Overself shine forth.

(24-4-93)

In contemplating deeply Nature's beauty around one, as some of us have done, it is possible to slip into a stillness where we realize that there never was a past but always the *NOW*—the ever-present timeless Consciousness—all peace, all harmony; that there is no past—just the eternal. Where are the shadows of negativity then? They are non-existent! This can happen if we forget the self, with its narrowed viewpoint, and surrender to the impersonal. In that brief experience there is no conflict to trouble the mind.

(19-4-184)

The seeker after stillness should be told that the stillness is always there. Indeed it is in every man. But he has to learn, first, to let it in and, second, how to do so. The first beginning of this is to remember. The second is to recognize the inward pull. For the rest, the stillness itself will guide and lead him to itself.   (24-4-51)

Continuous remembrance of the Stillness, accompanied by automatic entry into it, is the sum and substance of the Short Path, the key practice to success. At all times, under all circumstances, this is to be done. That is to say, it really belongs to and is part of the daily and ordinary routine existence. Consequently, whenever it is forgotten, the practitioner must note his failure and make instant correction. The inner work is kept up until it goes on by itself.   (23-6-210)

Every time he departs from the stillness there is needed a warning awareness. This does not easily or normally come by itself but by self-training, self-observation—"mindfulness," the Buddha called it. The feeling for it has to be persistently nurtured; first brought into being, then preserved at all hours of the day and in whatever surroundings he finds himself.   (23-6-234)

The spirit (Brahman) is NOT the stillness, but is found by humans who are in the precondition of stillness. The latter is their human reaction to Brahman's presence coming into *their* field of awareness.   (24-4-5)

By this simple act of unlearning all that you know—all that you have acquired by thinking, by remembrance, by measurements, by comparison, and by judgement—when you return to the mere emptying of the consciousness of its contents of thoughts and ideas, and when you come to the pure consciousness in itself, then only can you rest in the Great Silence.   (24-4-78)

Witness

His role is to play witness of what he is, how he behaves, the thoughts he admits, just as if he were witnessing someone else. This move-over from the actively-engaged person to the watcher who is impersonal and disengaged even in the midst of action, is one from drift to control. He must begin by putting the ego, his own ego, forward as an *object* of observation. He will not succeed fully in doing so, because he is involved on both sides—as subject and object—but the direction can be fixed and the work can be started. With time and practice, study and reflection, help and sincerity, some sort of impersonality and neutrality can be established. When inner stillness is fully reached, the work becomes much easier until it is completed by the grace of the higher Self, Overself. Of course, outside of meditation, he is conscious of his commonplace body; but he is also conscious of his awe-inspiring Overself. He sees the first as part of a passing show, himself as an uninvolved observer, and behind both the eternal Overself. (23-6-97)

To play the role of an observer of life, his own life, is to assist the process of inwardly detaching himself from it. And the field of observation must include the mental events, the thought-happenings, also. For mentalism shows that they are really one world. In the end everything belonging to experience belongs to mental experience. (23-6-82)

The passive submission to time keeps man enchained. The willed meditation on the infinite observer which is ever with him and within him is a revolt which weakens every link of his chains.

(*Wisdom of the Overself*, p. 352)

There would be no hope of ever getting out of this ego-centered position if we did not know these three things. First, the ego is only an accumulation of memories and a series of cravings, that is, thought; it is a fictitious entity. Second, the thinking activity can come to an end in stillness. Third, Grace, the radiation of the Power beyond man, is ever-shining and ever-present. If we let the mind become deeply still and deeply observant of the ego's self-preserving instinct, we open the door to Grace, which then lovingly swallows us. (8-4-417)

The practice of the impersonal point of view under the guidance of mentalism leads in time to the discovery that the ego is an image formed in the mind, mind-made, an image with which we have got inextricably intertwined. But this practice begins to untie us and set us free. (8-2-34)

All this implies that matter is also a myth, unreal. Still more it implies that the ego is a myth, illusory. Here, then, is the first practice of the ultimate path: think constantly of that Mind which is producing the ego, all the other egos around, and all the world, in fact. Keep this up until it becomes habitual. The consequence is that one tends in time to regard his own ego with complete detachment, as though he were regarding somebody else. Furthermore, it forces him to take the standpoint of the *all*, and to see unity as fundamental being. (excerpted from 21-3-88)

When a man has practised this exercise for some time and to some competency, he will become repeatedly aware of a curious experience. For a few minutes at most and often only for a few moments, he will seem to have stepped outside his body and to be confronting himself, looking at his own face as though it were someone else's. Or he will seem to be standing behind his own body and seeing his face from a side angle. This is an important and significant experience. (23-6-91)

The position of the impersonal observer is only a tentative one, assumed because it is a practical help perhaps midway toward the goal. For when it is well-established in understanding, outlook, and practice, something happens by itself: the observer and the observed ego with its body and world become swallowed up in the undivided Mind. (23-6-84)

Timeless Reality

The exercise of trying to break through the mystery of time, which is a mental state, into timelessness, which is not, belongs to the Short Path and is important, valuable, but admittedly difficult for beginners. It is practised by confining the thoughts again and again during spare moments and brief leisurely periods to the meaning of timelessness, of the eternal now, and of the everlasting Presence. (23-8-145)

The personal history which has gone before—let it really go and be free of the past, which can become a mental prison for unwary persons; learn to abide in the timeless, coming out of it as duties call but holding on to it as the background. (24-3-227)

Our best time occurs when we forget the passing of time. Here, for those who can appreciate it, is a clue to the nature of real happiness. (19-4-162)

It is in the fullness of the eternal present, the eternal now, that a person can really live happily. For by seeking That which makes him conscious of the present moment, by remembering it as being the essence of his fleeting experience, he completes that experience and fulfills its lofty purpose. (*Perspectives* 19-30)

How can we win this freedom of timelessness? There is one way and that is to step into the Void and to stay there. We must find, in short, the eternal *Now*. (23-8-114)

Wake from the Dream

One special exercise of the Short Path is easily done by some persons and gives them excellent results, although it is hard to do by others. It consists in refusing to let remain any particular mental registration of the surrounding place or people, or of any physical experience being undergone. Instead the mental image is to be firmly dismissed with the thought, "This too is like a dream," and then immediately forgotten. The exercise may be kept up for fifteen to twenty minutes at a time. The practical benefit it yields is to give improved self-control; the metaphysical benefit is to weaken the sway of illusion; the mystical benefit is to enable him to take the stand of the Witness-attitude more easily; and the personal benefit is to make him a freer and happier man.

(23-6-95)

Past, present, future become mere dreams when considered against the background of THAT. If man could switch his thought of self over to the Source, and keep on identifying it with that, his consciousness would be transformed. (24-3-240)

Mind the Breath

The would-be-illumined person must conform to the double action of nature in him: to the outgoing and incoming breaths. So his illumination, when it happens, must be *there* and *here*: in the mind and in the body. The two together form the equilibrium of the double life we are called upon to live: that is, being in the world and yet not being of it. In the prolongation of the expiring breath we not only get rid of negative thought but also of the worldliness, the materialism, of keeping to the physical interests alone. With the incoming breath we draw positive, inspiring remembrance of the divine hidden in the Void. Hence we are *there* in the mind and *here* in the body. We recognize the truth of eternity, the act in time. We see the reality of the Void, yet know that the entire Universe comes forth from it. (*Perspectives*-5-28)

Inspired Art

The exercises of sinking oneself in enjoyment of an artistic production constitute another Short Path method, provided they are followed up and completed by further stages described in the seventh and eighth chapters of *The Quest of the Overself.* These exercises will be useful only if the music, literature, or painting is truly inspired. (23-6-40)

Remembrance

No other act is so urgent or so important as this, to turn now in thought and remembrance, in love and aspiration, toward the Overself. For if you do not but turn toward that other and worldly act which is so clamant and demanding, you fall into a tension which may lead to error and consequent suffering. But if you do turn toward the Overself first and then act, you rise up to inner calm and consequent wiser judgement. (13-2-225)

Why should the Short Path be a better means of getting Grace than the Long one? There is not only the reason that it is not occupied with the ego but also that it continually keeps up remembrance of the Overself. It does this with a heart that gives, and is open to receive, love. It thinks of the Overself throughout the day. Thus, it not only comes closer to the source from which Grace is being perpetually radiated, but it also is repeatedly inviting Grace with each loving remembrance. (23-6-149)

One of the most valuable forms of yoga is the yoga of constant remembrance. Its subject may be a mystical experience, intuition, or idea. In essence it is really an endeavour to insert the transcendental atmosphere into the mundane life. (23-6-212)

The loving, adoring recollection of the Overself, the constant return to memory of it amid the world's distractions, the reiteration of this divine thought as a permanent background to all other thinking, is itself a yoga path. Indeed it is the same as that taught by Saint Paul when he wrote, "Pray without ceasing" and "Bring every thought into captivity to Jesus Christ." (23-6-237)

The best way to honour this immense truth of the ever-present reality of the Overself is to remember it—as often, as continuously, and as determinedly as possible. It is not only the best way but also the most rewarding one. For then its saving grace may bestow great blessing. (23-6-172)

Constant Remembrance Exercises: The Overself is a term of which past experience may furnish no meaning. But perhaps you have had strangely beautiful moments when everything seemed to be still, when an ethereal world of being seemed very near to you. Well, in those moments you were lifted up to the Overself. The task you should set yourself is to recapture that blessed presence and feel once again that beautiful interlude of unearthly stillness.

If, however, you cannot recall such moments or if, recalling them, you cannot regain afresh their vividness and reality, then there is an alternative path. Make it your business to recall the picture and presence of some man whom you believe is awake to his Overself-consciousness. Take him as your guru and therefore as an outstretched hand which you can mentally grasp and by which you can gradually lift yourself. Thus if the Overself is a vague abstraction to you, he, as a living person whom you have met, is not. He can easily be for you a definite focus of concentration, a positive point in the infinite to which you can direct your inward glance. (23-6-177)

The Glimpse is to be recalled frequently and enjoyed reminiscently. Let it help him in this way to dedicate the day to greater obedience of intuitive urge. Let it bring forth afresh that love of and aspiration toward the Overself which are necessary prerequisites to a stable experience of it. (22-5-31)

This seemingly simple exercise is of universal availability, for it can be done wherever he wishes and whenever he wishes. There is no moment which does not offer a chance to practise it, no situation in which it is not opportune. All that he has to do is to remember that he is a Quester, that he is also a divine being as well as an animal being, that he must act from his whole manhood and not merely from a fragment of it. But this remembrance is not to be struggled for; it is to be established as a natural habit and a relaxing one, whatever the tensions around him. The more he practises the more he can consolidate this way of life, this unique combination of acting in the world as if he knew nothing more than worldly demands and being within himself quite detached from the world. (23-6-239)

The Overself Remembrance Exercise

Name: It is so simple that it is called an exercise only for name's sake. In the beginning it requires effort just like any other practice.

How to:
1) To be practised at all times, in all places and under all bodily conditions. It consists of the constant loving recall to mind of the existence of, and his inner identity with, the Overself.

2) It involves the repeated and devoted recollection that there is this other and greater self, a warm, felt, living thing, overshadowing and watching over him.

3) It should be continued until he is able to keep the thought of the Overself as a kind of setting for all his other thoughts.

Glimpse:
If he has ever had a glimpse of a supersensuous higher existence which profoundly impressed him and perhaps led him to take to the quest, it is *most important* that he should also insert the remembrance of this experience into his exercise. He should try to bring as vividly as possible to his mind the sense of peace and exaltation which he then felt.

Warning:
One danger of this remembrance exercise is that it can become automatic too soon and thus merely mechanical and hollow. The remembrance must be a warm, felt, living thing if the spirit of the exercise is to be retained and not lost.

When to:
1) The inward concentration should persist behind and despite outward activity.

2) The Overself remembrance should be held in the back

of the mind, even though he may appear to be properly attentive to external matters.

3) He should keep the exercise always or as often as possible in the mind's background while paying attention to duties in the foreground.

4) Though the foreground of his consciousness is busy attending to the affairs of daily living, its background abides in a kind of sacred emptiness wherein no other thought may intrude than this thought of the Overself.

5) The remembrance should become the unmoved pivot upon which the pendulum of external activity swings perpetually to and fro.

Free time:

When he has free time, it should come to the fore. Every time there is relaxation from duties, he should let attention fly eagerly and more fully back to it.

How long:

He should train himself in this exercise:

1) until it becomes quite easy and effortless;

2) until this inward concentration has been set in habitual motion;

3) until the remembrance continues of its own accord;

4) until its practice has become firmly and successfully established as ceaseless flow;

5) until the loving recall to mind of the existence of, and his inner identity with, the Overself becomes constant;

6) until the practice is absorbed in perfect and perpetual performance;

7) until he experiences the Overself unceasingly as the unannounced and impersonal centre of his personal gravity.

Potency:

This method has a peculiar potency of its own despite its informal and unprogrammed character. Its unexpected effectiveness is therefore not to be measured by its obvious simplicity.

Grace:

When the remembrance becomes ceaseless flow, the Overself will bring him a remarkable fruitage of grace. When he turns habitually inwards toward the Overself, grace can operate more readily in all matters. When the grace starts working, this is likely to remove a number of internal and external obstacles in his path—sometimes in a seemingly miraculous manner—and eventually bring him to a truer self-awareness.

(23-6-176)

Until it is brought to his attention, he may not know that the idol at whose feet he is continually worshipping is the ego. If he could give to God the same amount of remembrance that he gives to his ego, he could quite soon attain, and become established in, that enlightenment to which other men devote lifetimes of arduous effort. (8-4-153)

By thought, the ego was made; by thought, the ego's power can be unmade. But the thought must be directed toward a higher entity, for the ego's willingness to attack itself is only a pretense. Direct it constantly to the Overself, be mentally devoted to the Overself, and emotionally love the Overself. Can it then refuse to help you? (18-1-77)

The basis of this exercise is that the remembering of the Overself leads in time to the forgetting of the ego. To let the mind dwell constantly on the thought of the Overself, tranquillizes it. To bring the figure of the spiritual guide into it, strengthens it. (23-6-152)

To keep up this remembrance all the time, in all circumstances, requires practice and perseverance to an extent that seems beyond the ordinary. But they are actually within everyone's untapped resources and untouched reserves. (23-6-244)

Fix the attention undividedly upon the Overself which is anchored in your heart-centre. Then everything you do during the day will naturally be divinely inspired action and true service. The Overself is your true source of power: turn towards it and receive its constructive guidance for your task of daily living. (23-6-165)

Whether his body finds itself among thieves or his mind finds itself among theories, the aspirant's duty of being *aware* ever remains paramount. He may work in the home, the office, or the field, and this activity should be quite compatible with holding on to the higher consciousness, through practice of this Recollection Exercise. The latter need not get in the way of his ordinary faculties or perceptions. (23-6-229)

He is wrong to object that you can't hold two different thoughts at the same time and that hence you can't remember God and attend to worldly details simultaneously. You can. God is not a thought, but an awareness on a higher level. Mind does not hold God. Certainly, mind can't have two objects of thought, for they are in duality, but they can be held by God's presence. Only here is the union of subject and object possible. All other thoughts are in duality. (23-6-256)

In remembrance, he should once again love the beauty and revere the solemnity of this experience. If the effort to remember the Overself is kept up again and again, it attenuates the materialistic mental tendencies inherited from former lives and arrests the natural restlessness of attention. It eventually achieves a mystical concentration of thoughts akin in character to that reached during set periods of meditation, but with the added advantage of not stopping the transaction of worldly activity.

Moments of utter inward stillness may come to him. The ordinary familiar ego will then desert him with a lightning-like suddenness and with hardly less brevity. Let him fix these moments firmly in his memory. They are to be used in the ensuing years as themes for meditation and goals for striving.

(23-6-186)

He must think as often and as intently of the Overself as an infatuated girl thinks of the next appointed meeting with her lover. His whole heart must be held captive, as it were, by this aspiration. This is to be practised not only at set formal times but also constantly throughout the day as an exercise in recollection. This yoga, done at all times and in all places, becomes a permanent life and not merely a transient exercise. This practice of constant remembrance of the Overself purifies the mind and gradually renders it naturally introverted, concentrates and eventually illumines it. (23-6-217)

This act of recollection requires no effort, no exercise of the power of will. It is an act of turning in, through and by the power of love, toward the source of being. Love redirects the attention and love keeps it concentrated, sustained, obedient. (23-6-255)

Although when feeling a descent of the stillness the aspirant is told to drop whatever he is doing and to hold himself in the stillness as long as he can or as long as it is there, he may also practise a useful exercise entirely on his own initiative at any time of the day involving a similar mental and physical posture. For this purpose he holds whatever he is doing whenever he wishes and as often as he wishes and keeps himself suspended, as it were, not moving, not thinking of anything else except the passive remembrance of the Overself. This special exercise of remembrance may be done for a single minute or for a few, just as he wishes. (23-6-200)

By keeping close to the Overself he can gain its protective guiding or helpful influence. No day should pass without its remembrance, no enterprise should be begun without its invocation.

(23-6-169)

If the past is unredeemable, and the future unpredictable, what more practical course is open than to safeguard the present by constant remembrance of the divine? (23-6-158)

He cultivates a more joyous attitude, this man on the Short Path, for remembrance of the Overself, which he practises constantly, reminds him of the glory of the Overself. (23-1-106)

No amount of exaggerated homage to a guru can take the place of remembering the Real. (23-6-156)

The successful philosopher is no dreamer: he keeps his practicality, his interest in world affairs, his willingness to accept responsibility, thus remaining an effective servant of mankind. But all this is done *within* the Remembrance. (23-6-242)

"As If" Identity Exercise

Better than any long-drawn yoga discipline is the effort to rivet one's hold on the here-and-now of one's divinity. (23-5-175)

This then is the ultimate truth—that in our inmost nature we are anchored in God, inseparable from God, and that the discovery of this heavenly nature is life's loftiest purpose. Even now, already, today, we are as divine as we ever shall be. The long evolutionary ladder which by prophets and teachers, gurus and guides we are bidden to climb toilsomely and slowly and painfully need not be climbed at all if only we heed this truth continually, if we refuse to let it go, if we make it ours in all parts of our being—in thought, feeling, faith, and action. (23-1-6)

A valuable practice of the Short Path is to *see* himself already enjoying the realization of its goal, already partaking of its glorious rewards. This is a visualizing exercise in which his own face confronts him, a smiling triumphant face, a calm peaceful face. It is to be done as many times every day as he can remember to do it. (23-6-50)

A part of the practical technique for attaining the inner awareness of this timeless reality is the practice of the AS IF exercise. With some variations it has already been published in *The Wisdom of the Overself,* and an unpublished variant has been included in descriptions of the Short Path as "identification with the Overself." The practitioner regards himself no longer from the standpoint of the quester, but from that of the Realized Man. He assumes, in thought and action, that he has nothing to attain because he bases himself on the Vedantic truth that Reality, of which he is a part, is here and now—is not reached in Time, being timeless—and that therefore he is as divine as he ever will be. He rejects the *appearance* of things, which identifies man only with his ego, and insists on the higher identification with Overself also.

(23-6-115)

On this Short Path he searches into the meaning of Being, of being himself and of being-in-itself, until he finds its finality. Until this search is completed, he accepts the truth, passed down to him by the Enlightened Ones, that in his inmost essence he is Reality. This leads to the logical consequence that he should disregard personal feelings which continue from past tendencies, habits, attitudes, and think and act as if he were himself an enlightened one! For now he knows by evidence, study, and reflection that the Overself is behind, and is the very source of, his ego, just as he knows by the experience of feeling during his brief Glimpses. Bringing this strong conviction into thought and act and attitude is the "Heavenly Way" [or "As If"] exercise, a principal one on the Short Path.

He pretends to be what he aims to become: thinks, speaks, acts, behaves as a master of emotion, desire, ego because he would be one. But he should play this game for, and to, himself alone, not to enlarge himself in others' eyes, lest he sow the seed of a great vanity. (23-6-109)

Identity Exercise: He will not have to struggle as on the Long Path. There will no more be irksome effort. The mind will be glad to rest in this positive state, if he holds from the very beginning the faith that it already is accomplished, that the aspiration toward it is being fulfilled *now*, not at some unknown distant time. Such an attitude engenders something more than pleasant feelings of hope and optimism: it engenders subconscious power. (23-6-131)

He shapes himself into another person in imagination, in faith, and in will. For a while he creates the illusion of a new destiny accompanying this new person. Is this not a veritable rebirth? Does he not get away from the old everyday person and forget him utterly through this miraculous transformation? He lives so completely in this visualized ideal self that there is no space left for the old faults, the old weaknesses to creep in. (23-6-144)

He learns that he may set his own limits, that so long as he thinks all day that he is only this person, doing and speaking in the ordinary way what men usually do, then he is certainly nothing more. But if he starts the day on a higher level, thinking that he is divine in his inmost being, and keeps on that level as the hours pass, then he will feel closer to it. This is a practical procedure, one which has its effect on consciousness, on character, and on events. (23-6-128)

The method of the Short Path is to affirm that in the heavenly consciousness of the Overself there is no evil, no wrong-doing, no sinfulness, and no faultiness; and that because the true being of man is there the aspirant should identify himself with it in faith, thought, and vision. In that threefold way he sees himself dwelling and acting in the Overself, and therefore without his specific sins and faults. He regards them as non-existent and drops anxiety or concern about them. He does this as much as he can from morning to night and this fulfils Jesus' injunction to "pray without ceasing" in a deeper and philosophical sense.
(23-6-129)

This practice in the Short Path of self-identification with the Overself is to be done both casually at odd moments and deliberately at daily contacts in meditation. It is through them—whenever the identification is effectual—that Grace gets some of its chance to work its transformation upon him. (23-6-118)

It is a vision of himself as he could be but transferred from future possibility to present actualization. This "Identity" exercise rightly belongs to the Short Path, for in the case of a beginner, whose knowledge is small, efforts limited, and character unpurified, its practice could be self-deceptive. (23-6-143)

The "Identity" exercise is a changeover from humbly aspiring to a higher level to creatively imagining oneself as being there already. The dangers here are conceit, deceit, and complacency.

(23-6-142)

The "As If" exercise is not merely pretense or make-believe. It requires penetrative study and sufficient understanding of the high character and spiritual consciousness in the part to be played, the role to be enacted, the auto-suggestion to be realized.

(23-6-113)

This practice of picturing oneself as one ought to be, of visualizing the man free from negative qualities and radiant with positive ones that are part of the Quest's ideal, has near-magical results.

(23-6-123)

To practise the "As If" Short Path exercise successfully, it is necessary to let go and forget all past techniques and begin afresh; they are attachments and, to that extent, distractions. They may cause self-consciousness, anxiety for success, and impatience. The divinity is there, within you; have faith that it *is* so and entrust yourself to it.

(23-6-138)

Practice of the "As If" exercise is like being spiritually reborn and finding a new way of life. It gives courage to those who feel grievously inadequate, hope to those who feel hooked by their past failures.

(23-6-111)

To practise the "As If" Short Path exercise successfully, it is necessary to let go and forget all past techniques and begin afresh; they are attachments and, to that extent, distractions. They may cause self-consciousness, anxiety for success, and impatience. The divinity is there, within you; have faith that it *is* so and entrust yourself to it.

(23-6-138)

Even if it only be a pose that is cultivated, it still remains a valuable discipline and exercise which gives good results. For it has much suggestive power, this "As If" method, and is an essential part of the Short Path. (23-6-147)

Into the Void

Meditation on the void has, as one of its chief aims, the overcoming of egoism. It not only destroys the narrow view of self but sublimates the very thought of self into the thought of pure unbounded existence. Employed at the proper time and not prematurely, it burns up the delusion of separateness. (23-8-158)

Remove the concept of the ego from a man and you remove the solid ground from beneath his feet. A yawning abyss seems to open up under him. It gives the greatest fright of his life, accompanied by feelings of utter isolation and dreadful insecurity. He will then clamour urgently for the return of his beloved ego and return to safety once more—unless his determination to attain truth is so strong and so exigent that he can endure the ordeal, survive the test, and hold on until the Overself's light irradiates the abyss. (8-5-465)

It is not essential to enter the trance state in order to experience sufficient depth of meditation, although many do seek it in the popular belief of its necessity. The advanced Short Path treader develops the capacity without the necessity. That is to say, he can enjoy the benefits of a stilled mind in an instant whenever outer circumstances permit him to relax but without having to fall into a condition oblivious of outside scenes, sounds, and shapes. (23-1-148)

The highest and the last of the inward-bound stages is still to be reached, and this is the self-knowing Void of Being which can repeat the phrase "I am that I am" of Exodus 3:14, but which is without any other predicate. (23-8-3)

Not until the ego is completely deflated and falls into the Void will he know, feel, and fully realize the blissfulness of salvation.

(8-4-447)

At this point he gets so lost in the Void that he forgets who it is who is meditating. Then and thus he receives a further answer to the question "Who am I?" (23-8-100)

When all action comes to an end, when the body is immobile and the consciousness stilled, there is achieved what the Chinese have called Wu Wei, meaning non-doing. This brings a wonderful peace, for tied up with it is non-desiring and non-aspiring. The quester has then come close to the end, but until this peace is thoroughly and permanently established in him, the quest must go on. Let go of all negative thoughts, especially those which concern others. Cease from condemnation and criticism except where it is a necessary part of one's obligation, duty, or position in the world, such as a magistrate's. (24-3-289)

Through repeated contemplation of the void, the mind rids itself of the illusions of matter time space and personality and eventually the truth is reached. (23-8-114)

Why be afraid of this declaration: that the final goal is to merge in the Absolute? Is it because it promises the same as death—annihilation? Yet whenever deep sleep is entered this merger happens. The ego with its thoughts, desires, and agitations, is gone; the world, with its relativities, is no more. Time, space, form, memory are lost. Yet all reappears next morning. So it is not a real death. It is pure Being. Meditation tries to reproduce this condition, to achieve a return to deep sleep but with the added factor of *awareness*. In the final phase—*Nirvikalpa Samadhi*—it succeeds. Man dissolves but his divine Source remains as the residue, as what he always and basically was. This is why philosophy includes meditation. (4-1-199)

It would be completely false to regard the Void as being a nothing and containing nothing. It is Being itself, and contains reality behind all things. Nor is it a kind of inertia, of paralysis. All action springs out of it, all the world-forces derive from it. (28-1-118)

We must withdraw every thing and thought from the mind except this single thought of trying to achieve the absence of what is not the Absolute. This is called *Gnana Yoga: "Neti, Neti"* (It is not this), as Shankara called it. And he must go on with this negative elimination until he reaches the stage where a great Void envelops him. If he can succeed in holding resolutely to this Void in sustained concentration—and he will discover it is one of the hardest things in the world to do so—he will abruptly find that it is not a mere mental abstraction but something real, not a dream but the most concrete thing in his experience. Then and then only can he declare positively, "It is *This*." For he has found the Overself. (23-8-118)

A further result of this contemplation of the world as the great Void is that the work done by mentalistic study is advanced still further, for not only are the things experienced by the five senses seen to be only thoughts but the thoughts themselves are now seen to be the transient spume and spray flung out of seeming

Emptiness. Thus there is a complete reorientation from thoughts to Thought. Instead of holding a single thought or scenes of ideas in perfect concentration, the practiser must now move away from all ideas altogether to that seeming emptiness in which they arise. And the latter, of course, is the pure, passive, undifferentiated mind-stuff out of which the separate ideas are produced. Here there is no knowing and discriminating between one idea and another, no stirring into consciousness of this and that, but rather a sublime vacancy. For the Mind-essence is not something which we can picture to ourselves; it is utterly formless. It is as empty and as ungraspable as space.   (23-8-115)

The final grade of inner experience, the deepest phase of contemplation, is one where the experiencer himself disappears, the meditator vanishes, the knower no longer has an object—not even the Overself—to know for duality collapses. Because this grade is beyond the supreme "Light" experience where the Overself reveals its presence visually as a dazzling mass, shaft, ball, or ray of unearthly radiance which is seen whether the bodily eyes are open or closed, it has been called the divine darkness.   (28-2-147)

Repose in this condition of vast emptiness is accompanied by intense and vivid happiness. He knows that he is with the living God. He understands that he has come as close to God as it is possible for a human being on earth to do and yet remain human and alive. But he knows and understands all this not by the movement of ideas—for there are none here—but by a feeling which captures his whole being. But it is during this final experience of the Void, when he passes beyond all relativity, that he experiences Mind to be the only reality, the only enduring existence, and that all else is but a shadow. Entry into this stage is therefore a critical point for every aspirant.   (23-8-32)

Hidden behind every particular thought there exists the divine element which makes possible our consciousness of that thought. If therefore we seek that element, we must seek it first by widening the gap between them and then dissolving all thoughts, and second by contemplating that out of which they have arisen.

(23-8-159)

During the gap—infinitesimal though it be—between two thoughts, the ego vanishes. Hence it may truly be said that with each thought it reincarnates anew. There is no real need to wait for the series of long-lived births to be passed through before liberation can be achieved. The series of momentary births also offers this opportunity, provided a man knows how to use it.

(23-8-162)

There are certain intervals of consciousness between two thoughts—such as those between waking and sleep and those between sleep and waking—which normally pass unobserved because of the rapidity and brevity associated with them. Between one moment and another there is the timeless consciousness; between one thought and another there is a thought-free consciousness. It is upon this fact that a certain exercise was included in *The Wisdom of the Overself* which had not previously been published in any Western book. But it is not a modern discovery. It was known to the ancient Egyptians, it was known to the Tibetan occultists, and in modern times it was probably known to Krishnamurti. The Egyptians, preoccupied as they were with the subject of death and the next world, based their celebrated *Book of the Dead* upon it. *The Tibetan Book of the Dead* contained the same theme. Between the passing out of the invisible vital-forces body at the end of each incarnation and its entry into that state of consciousness which is death, the same interval reappears. If the dying man can lift himself up to it, seize upon it, and not let it escape him, he will then enter into heaven—the true heaven. And it was to remind him of this fact and to help him achieve this feat that the ancient priests attended his last moments and chanted the pertinent passages from these books. This mysterious interval makes its appearance throughout life and even at death, and yet men notice it not and miss an opportunity. It happens not only at the entry into death but also in between two breaths. It is possible to go even further and say that the interval reappears for a longer period between two incarnations for there is then the blocking out of all impressions of the past prior to taking on a new body. Plato must have known it. (23-6-81)

The succession of thoughts appears in time, but the gap between two of them is outside time. The gap itself is normally unobserved. The chance of enlightenment is missed. (23-8-163)

It is the presence of the physical ego in the wakeful state that paralyses all spiritual awareness therein. It is the absence of the personal and physical ego in the deep sleep state that paralyses all material awareness therein, too. By keeping it out and yet keeping in wakefulness, the transcendental consciousness is able to provide the requisite condition for an unbroken spiritual awareness that is not only superior to the three states but continues its own existence behind theirs. (19-3-180)

They may come quite abruptly, those intensely lived moments of true vision, those spasmodic glimpses of a beauty and truth above the best which earthly life offers. The mind then rests and there is a gap in its usual activities, a Void out of which these heavenly experiences come to life as they overcome our ordinary feelings. (22-6-28)

Students draw back affrighted at the concept of a great void which leaves them nothing, human or divine, to which they may cling. How much the more will they draw back, not from a mere concept, but from an actual experience through which they must personally pass! Yet this is an event, albeit not the final one on the ultimate ultramystic path, which they can neither avoid nor evade. It is a trial which must be endured, although to the student who has resigned himself to acceptance of the truth whatever face it bears—who has consequently comprehended already the intellectual emptiness of both Matter and Personality—this experience will not assume the form of a trial but rather of an adventure. After such a rare realization, he will emerge a different man. Henceforth he will know that nothing that has shape, nobody who bears a form, no voice save that which is soundless can ever help him again. He will know that his whole trust, his whole hope, and his whole heart are now and forevermore to be surrendered unconditionally to this Void which mysteriously will no longer be a Void for him. For it is God.   (23-8-43)

The first contact of the student with the Void will probably frighten him. The sense of being alone—a disembodied spirit—in an immense abyss of limitless space gives a kind of shock to him unless he comes well prepared by metaphysical understanding and well fortified by a resolve to reach the supreme reality. His terror is, however, unjustified. In the act of projecting the personal ego the Overself has necessarily to veil itself from the ego at the same time. Thus ignorance is born.   (23-8-35)

Those who find that beyond the Light they must pass through the Void, the unbounded emptiness, often draw back affrighted and refuse to venture farther. For here they have naught to gain or get, no glorious spiritual rapture to add to their memories, no great power to increase their sense of being a co-worker with God. Here their very life-blood is to be squeezed out as the price of entry; here they must become the feeblest of creatures. (23-8-59)

So many mystics are quite unnecessarily frightened by this concept of the Void that it is necessary to reassure them. They halt on the very threshold of their high attainment and go no farther, because they fear they will be extinguished, annihilated. The truth is that this will happen only to their lower nature. They themselves will remain very much alive. Thus it is not the best part of their nature which really dreads the experience of the Void, but the worst part. (23-8-57)

What is called *Turiya* or the "fourth state" in Sanskrit, although it is neither waking, dreaming, nor sleeping, is related however to all three as their background. Therefore, before one falls asleep it comes into play. Before one wakes up in the morning it also comes into play. Or before a dream comes to an end and deep sleep supervenes, it comes into play. This is why either the practice of meditation or the brief practice of spiritual remembrance at any of these three natural pause periods takes the fullest advantage of them. This is also why during the interval between two separate thoughts, it comes into play. Thus, throughout a man's life, he's comfortably being brought back into touch with his divine Self. But because his face is turned the other way and he's looking in the wrong direction, he never takes advantage and becomes aware of that Self. (19-3-196)

Beyond the Short Path

Those who look for advancement by looking for inner experiences or for discoveries of new truth do well. But they need to understand that all this is still personal, still something that concerns the ego even if it be the highest and best part of the ego. Their greatest advance will be made when they cease holding the wish to make any advance at all, cease this continual looking at themselves, and instead come to a quiet rest in the simple fact that God is, until they live in this fact alone. That will transfer their attention from self to Overself and keep them seeing its presence in everyone's life and its action in every event. The more they succeed in holding to this insight, the less will they ever be troubled or afraid or perplexed again; the more they recognize and rest in the divine character, the less will they be feverishly concerned about their own spiritual future. (23-5-222)

The limitation of the Long Path is that it is concerned only with thinning down, weakening, and reducing the ego's strength. It is not concerned with totally deflating the ego. Since this can be done only by studying the ego's nature metaphysically, seeing its falsity, and recognizing its illusoriness, which is not even done by the Short Path, then all the endeavours of the Short Path to practise self-identification with the Overself are merely using imagination and suggestion to create a new mental state that, while imitating the Overself's state, does not actually transcend the ego-mind but exists within it still. So a third phase becomes necessary, the phase of getting rid of the ego altogether; this can be done only by the final dissolving operation of Grace, which the man has to request and to which he has to give his consent. To summarize the entire process, the Long Path leads to the Short Path, and the Short Path leads to the Grace of an unbroken egoless consciousness. (23-5-206)

There has to be life, feeling. The amount of Long Path and Short Path depends on the individual. If you don't know, you must ask your guru. It seems complicated, and in a way it is. But in a way, it is very simple.

In the end you will reject both. There is no Long Path or Short Path. We have constructed them to conform to what we think. Buddha says in the *Dhammapada* that you yourself made up this picture you have of yourself, the picture you think is real. It is made by thought and can be undone by thought.

You could also say there is nothing to the whole thing: simply surrender yourself to God. This is true if you can do it.

(excerpted from 23-5-56)

We who honour philosophy so highly cannot afford to be other than honest with ourselves. We have to acknowledge that the end of all our striving is surrender. No human being can do other than this—an utterly humble prostration, where we dissolve, lose the ego, lose ourselves—the rest is paradox and mystery.

(20-5-11)

9

Experiences Along the Way

Grace is of two kinds. The ordinary, better known, and inferior kind is that which is found on the Long Path. It flows from the Overself in automatic response to intense faith or devotion, expressed during a time of need. It is a reaction to seeking for help. The rarer and superior kind is found on the Short Path. It arises from self-identification with the Overself or constant recollection of it. There is no ego here to seek help or to call for a Grace which is necessarily ever present in the Overself.

(23-6-7)

There are little graces, such as those which produce the glimpse; but there is only one great Grace: this produces a lasting transformation, a deep radical healing and permanent enlightenment.

(18-5-13)

Ecstasy is not a permanent mark of the mystical experience, but only a temporary mark which accompanies its first discovery. It is the beginners who are so excited by mystical ecstasies, not the proficients. The process of re-adjusting the personality to a future filled with wonderful promise and stamped with tremendous importance naturally moves the emotional nature towards an extreme of delight. Nevertheless, it would be a mistake to regard the mystic's ecstasy as something that was merely emotional only. Behind it there is the all-important contribution of the Overself's grace, love, and peace. When the emotional excitement of the discovery eventually subsides, these will then show themselves more plainly as being its really significant elements.   (22-7-111)

The Timing of the Timeless

Whoever has been led into the cave of timeless life will poise his pen in a futile attempt to find words which will accurately measure this sublime experience. He rises renewed from the exquisite embrace of such a contemplation. He learns in those shining hours. That which he has been seeking so ardently has been within himself all the time. For there at the core of his being, hidden away underneath all the weakness, passion, pettiness, fear, and ignorance, dwells light, love, peace, and truth. The windows of his heart open on eternity, only he has kept them closed! He is as near the sacred spirit of God as he ever shall be, but he must open his eyes to see it. Man's divine estate is there deep within himself. But he must claim it.   (22-3-3)

There is no single path to enlightenment. Yoga has no monopoly. Life itself is the great enlightener. I met a man once who, after the shock of hearing his wife tell him that she had ceased to love him, that she had for some time had a secret lover, and that she requested a divorce so as to be able to marry him, felt a collapse of all his hitherto confidently held values and beliefs. For some days he was so affected that he could not eat. But his mind by then had become so extraordinarily lucid concerning these matters and himself, that he experienced moments of truth. Through them he came into a great peace and understanding, an inner change. What was the morning sun which awakened him? He did no yogic exercises, entered no churches, was too intent on his worldly business to read spiritual books. This brings me back to the theme: do not submit to the pressure of those who say there is only a single way to salvation (the way they follow or teach) do not let the mind be trammelled or narrowed. The truth is that the ways are many, are spread out in all directions, are individual. (1-5-209)

The truth may not always burst on its votary in a sudden brief and total flash. It may also come so slowly that he will hardly know its movement. But in both cases this progress will be measured by his abandonment of a purely personal and self-centered attitude towards life. (20-4-89)

Does enlightenment come all of a sudden? Or do we have to work slowly for it by degrees? The answer varies with the case concerned. Most need time to fit and equip themselves for the glorious moment of insight, but a few receive it in a day. It must be remembered that it does not actually happen in time but out of it, in the great Stillness. The man does not *know* the absolute final truth a second before—and then it is all there. How soon it can settle down in him will also vary with different persons—it was a few hours in one case but three years in another. (25-2-53)

When he feels the gentle coming of the presence of the higher self, at this point he must train himself in the art of keeping completely passive. He will discover that it is endeavouring actually to ensoul him, to take possession of him as a disembodied spirit is supposed to take possession of a living medium. His task now is purely negative; it is to offer no resistance to the endeavour but to let it have the fullest possible sway over him. The preliminary phases of his progress are over. Hitherto it was mostly his own efforts upon which he had to rely. Now, however, it is the Overself which will be the active agent in his development. All that is henceforth asked of him is that he remain passive, otherwise he may disturb the holy work by the interference of his blind ignorant self-will. His advance at this point no longer depends on his own striving. (2-9-30)

Once the Overself is felt in the heart as a living presence, it raises the consciousness out of the grip of the egoistic-desire parts of our being, frees it from the ups and downs of mood and emotion which they involve. It provides a sense of inner satisfaction that is complete in itself and irrespective of outside circumstances.

(22-3-104)

Enlightenment may come suddenly to a man, but then it is usually a temporary glimpse. Only rarely does it stay and never leave him. The normal way is a gradual one. The experience of Ramana Maharshi, Atmananda, and Aurobindo illustrates this rare fated exception, and can only be looked for at the risk of frustration.

(22-8-7)

If you believe that you have had the ultimate experience, it is more likely that you had an emotional, or mental, or mystic one. The authentic thing does not *enter* consciousness. You do not know that it has transpired. You discover it is already here only by looking back at what you were and contrasting it with what you now are; or when others recognize it in you and draw attention to it; or when a situation arises which throws up your real status. It is a permanent fact, not a brief mystic "glimpse." (28-2-139)

A mystic experience is simply something which comes and goes, whereas philosophic insight, once established in a man, cannot possibly leave him. He understands the Truth and cannot lose this understanding any more than an adult can lose his adulthood and become an infant. (20-4-198)

What are the signs whereby he shall know that this is an authentic glimpse of reality? First, it is and shall remain ever present. There is no future in it and no past. Second, the pure spiritual experience comes without excitement, is reported without exaggeration, and needs no external authority to authenticate it.

(22-7-199)

The glimpse, because it is situated between the mental conditions which exist before and afterwards, necessarily involves striking— even dramatic—contrast with their ordinariness. It seems to open on to the ultimate light-bathed height of human existence. But this experience necessarily provokes a human reaction to it, which is incorporated into the glimpse itself, becomes part of it. The permanent and truly ultimate enlightenment is pure, free from any admixture of reaction, since it is calm, balanced, and informed.

(25-2-27)

Mostly as a result of meditation, but sometimes during an unexpected glimpse, a mystical experience of an unusual kind may develop. He feels transparent to the Overself; its light passes into and through him. He then finds that his ordinary condition was as if a thick wall surrounded him, devoid of windows and topped by a thick roof, a condition of imprisonment in limitation and ordinariness. But now the walls turn to glass, their density is miraculously gone, he is not only open to the light streaming in but lets it pass on, irradiating the world around.   (22-6-166)

Ramana Maharshi had no Long Path experience at all; he practised no techniques; yet he was permanently enlightened at an early age. There are two lessons in this event. First, without either a Long or Short Path previous history a man may still find himself in the higher consciousness. This shows that Grace alone is a sufficient cause. Second, aside from the feeling of disgust with the world through failure to pass his school examinations, the only preparation which Maharshi underwent was falling involuntarily and profoundly into the trance state for three days. Here he was "pulled in" away from the senses and outer awareness by a strong force. This shows that *depth* of inner penetration of the mind's layers and *length* of period that contact is held with the Overself are the two important governors of the result attained. Go as deep as you can; stay there as long as you can; this seems to be the silent message of the Maharshi's own experience.   (25-3-76)

Pain and Loss

The place where you are, the people who surround you, the problems you encounter, and the happenings that take place just now—all have their special meaning for you. They come about under the law of recompense as well as under the particular needs of your spiritual growth. Study them well but impersonally, egolessly, and adjust your reactions accordingly. This will be hard and perhaps even unpalatable, yet it is the certain way to solving all your problems. This is what Jesus meant when he declared, "If any man will come after me, let him deny himself, and take up his cross daily, and follow me." This is that crucifixion of the ego which is true Christianity and which leads directly to the resurrection in the reality of the Overself. Regard your worst, most irritating trouble as the voice of your Overself. Try to hear what It says. Try to remove the obstructions It is pointing to within yourself. Look on this special ordeal, this particular trial, as having the most important significance in your own spiritual growth. The more crushing it is, the more effort is being made to draw you nearer to the Overself. At every point of your life, from one event, situation, contact to another, the Infinite Intelligence provides you with the means of growth, if only you will get out of the egoistic rut and take them. (2-4-24)

The upward flights of the aspirant's novitiate are bought at the cost of downward falls. It is as much a part of his experience of this quest to be deprived at times of all feeling that the divine exists and is real, as it is to have the sunny assurance of it.

At first the experience of reality comes only in flashes. Actually it is not the higher self which tantalizingly appears and disappears before the aspirant's gaze in this way, causing him alternating conditions of happy fruition and miserable sterility, but the higher self's loving Grace. Each time this is shed, the aspirant's first reaction is a strong sense of spiritual lack, dryness, darkness, and longing. This brings much unhappiness, self-discontent, and frustration. But it also brings both increased and intensified aspiration for the unearthly and distaste for the earthly. This phase passes away, however, and is followed by one as illuminative as the other was dark, as joyous as the other was unhappy, as productive as the other was barren, and as close to reality as the other seemed far from it. In that sacred presence a purifying process takes place. The old familiar and faulty self drops away like leaves from a tree in autumn. He makes the radiant discovery in his heart of its original goodness. But alas, when the presence departs, the lower self returns and resumes sovereignty. The period of illumination is often followed by a period of darkness. A spiritual advance which comes unexpectedly is usually succeeded by a period of recoil. Jubilation is followed by depression.

A greater trial still awaits him. The Overself demands a sacrifice upon its altar so utter, so complete that even the innocent natural longing for personal happiness must be offered up. As no novice and few intermediates could bear this dark night of the soul, and as even proficients cannot bear it without murmuring, it is reserved for the last group alone—which means that it happens at an advanced stage along the path, between a period of great illumination, and another of sublime union.

During this period the mystic will feel forsaken, emotionally fatigued and intellectually bored to such a degree that he may become a sick soul. Meditation exercises will be impossible and fruitless, aspirations dead and uninviting. A sense of terrible loneliness will envelop him. Interest in the subject may fall away or the feeling that further progress is paralysed may become dominant. Yet in spite of contrary appearances, this is all part of his development, which has taken a turn that will round it out and make it fuller. Most often the student is plunged into new types of experience during the dark period. The Overself sends him forth to endure tests and achieve balance.

The most dangerous feature of the "dark night" is a weakening of the will occurring at the same time as a reappearance of old forgotten evil tendencies. This is the point where the aspirant is really being tested, and where a proportion of those who have reached this high grade fail in the test and fall for several years into a lower one.

Even Muhammed had to undergo this experience of the dark night of the soul. It lasted three years and not a single illumination or revelation came to brighten his depressed heart. Indeed he even considered the idea of killing himself to put an end to it; and yet his supreme realization and world-shaking task were still ahead of him.

He who has passed through this deepest and longest of the "dark nights" which precedes mature attainment can never again feel excessive emotional jubilation. The experience has been like a surgical operation in cutting him off from such enjoyments. Moreover, although his character will be serene always, it will be also a little touched by that melancholy which must come to one who not only has plumbed the depths of life's anguish himself, but also has been the constant recipient of other people's tales of sorrow.

The aspirant can rest in the passive self-absorbed state for a short time only, for a few hours at most. The relentless dictates of Nature compel him to return to his suppressed ordinary state of active life.

This intermittent swinging to and fro between rapt self-absorption and the return to ordinary consciousness will tantalize him until he realizes what is the final goal. It will end only when his egoism has ended. Up to now he has succeeded in overcoming it fully in the contemplative state only. He must now overcome it in his ordinary active state. But the ego will not leave him here unless the purpose of its own evolution has been fulfilled. Therefore he must complete its all-round development, bring it to poise and balance, and then renounce it utterly. With the ego's complete abnegation, perfect, unbroken, and permanent oneness with the Overself ensues.   (23-3-1)

By freeing himself largely of attachments—and especially the subtlest yet largest of all, attachment to the ego—his heart is emptied. Into the void thus created, Grace can flow. Mystics who complain of the soul's dark night are led to know that it is a process whereby this space in the heart is being increased, a crushing of self into dust, to make room for Grace. If they are thus led to nothingness, let them remember that the Overself is no-thing.   (23-3-57)

The World as Illusion Is a Step

The world is neither an illusion nor a dream but is analogically *like* both. It is true that the mystics or yogis do experience it as such. This is a step forward toward liberation but must not be mistaken for liberation itself. When they pass upward to the higher or philosophic stage they will discover that all is Mind, whether the latter be creatively active or latently passive; that the world is, in its essential stuff, this Mind although its particular forms are transient and mortal; and that therefore there is no real difference between earthly experience and divine experience. Those who are wedded to forms, that is, appearances, set up such a difference and posit spirit and matter, *nirvana* and *samsara*, Brahman and Maya, and so forth, as antithetic opposites, but those who have developed insight perceive the essential stuff of everything even while they perceive its forms; hence they see all as *One*. It is as if a dreamer were to know that he was dreaming and thus understand that all the dream scenes and figures were nothing but one and the same stuff—his mind—while not losing his dream experience.   (21-3-24)

He must not let the *Ashtavakra Samhita* be misunderstood. It does not preach mystic idleness and indifference. The world is there for both sage and student, and both must work and serve— the difference being mental only. Illusionism is not the doctrine except as an intermediate stage towards truth, which is higher. One must participate in God's work by assisting evolution and redeeming the world, not squat idly in peace alone.   (19-1-57)

The *Advaitin* who declares that as such he has no point of view, has already adopted one by calling himself an Advaitin and by rejecting every other point of view as being dualistic. A human philosophy is neither dualistic alone nor nondualistic alone. It perceives the connection between the dream and the dreamer, the Real and the unreal, the consciousness and the thought. It accepts Advaita, but refuses to stop with it; it accepts duality, but refuses to remain limited to it; therefore it alone is free from a dogmatic point of view. But in attempting to bring into harmony that which forever is and that which is bound by time and space, it becomes a truly human philosophy of Truth. (20-1-478)

The mind passes through a stage when, seeking after truth, it finds out that the world is other than it seems to be, and that its material substance is not matter at all but energy: its form is illusory. But this is not the end. For the seeker does not stop there; if he proceeds farther, he may find that illusion is itself an illusion. It is next found to be derived from reality and to be a form assumed by reality. This is the sage's enlightenment, this is his experience. (25-2-229)

Intuition

The intuition must lead all the rest of man's faculties. He must follow it even when they do not agree with its guidance. For it sees farther than they ever can, being an efflux from the godlike part of himself which is in its way a portion of the universal deity. If he can be sure that it is not pseudo-intuition, truth in it will lead him to life's best, whether spiritual or worldly. (22-1-246)

Being guided intuitively does not mean that every problem will be solved instantly as soon as it appears. Some solutions will not come into consciousness until almost the very last minute before they are actually needed. He learns to be patient, to let the higher power take its own course. (22-1-180)

The intuitively governed mind is the undivided mind. It does not have to choose between contrasts or accept one of two alternatives. It does not suffer from the double-facedness of being swayed this way or that by conflicting evidence, contradictory emotions, or hesitant judgements.   (22-1-257)

It is a state of pure intelligence but without the working of the intellectual and ideational process. Its product may be named intuition. There are no automatically conceived ideas present in it, no habitually followed ways of thinking. It is pure, clear, stillness.   (22-3-204)

The unfulfilled future is not to be made an object of anxious thought or joyous planning. The fact that he has taken the tremendous step of offering his life in surrender to the Overself precludes it. He must now and henceforth let that future take care of itself, and await the higher will as it comes to him bit by bit. This is not to be confounded with the idle drifting, the apathetic inertia of shiftless, weak people who lack the qualities, the strength, and the ambition to cope with life successfully. The two attitudes are in opposition.

The true aspirant who has made a positive turning-over of his personal and worldly life to the care of the impersonal and higher power in whose existence he fully believes, has done so out of intelligent purpose, self-denying strength of will, and correct appraisal of what constitutes happiness. What this intuitive guidance of taking or rejecting from the circumstances themselves means in lifting loads of anxiety from his mind only the actual experience can tell. It will mean also journeying through life by single degrees, not trying to carry the future in addition to the present. It will be like crossing a river on a series of stepping-stones, being content to reach one at a time in safety and to think of the others only when they are progressively reached, and not before. It will mean freedom from false anticipations and useless planning, from vainly trying to force a path different from that ordained by God. It will mean freedom from the torment of not knowing what to do, for every needed decision, every needed choice, will become plain and obvious to the mind just as the time for it nears. For the intuition will have its chance at last to supplant the ego in such matters. He will no longer be at the mercy of the latter's bad qualities and foolish conceit.

(18-4-145)

Insight

Intuition knows earthly truth without the intervention of reasoning, while insight knows divine truth in the same direct way.

(20-4-151)

When the mystery of it all is solved, not merely intellectually but in experience, not only in the person himself but in transcending it, not only in the depth of meditation but in the world of activity; when this answer is richly felt as Presence and God, clearly known as Meaning and Mind, then, if he were to speak he would exclaim: "Thus It Is!" But this is not the beginner's glimpse: it is the sage's settled insight.

(25-2-24)

We need to know the truth, the wisdom-knowledge, but it is not enough. We need to have the living mystic experience, the vital feeling of what I am, but it is not enough. For we need to synthesize the two in a full actual intuitive realization, conferred by the Overself. This is Grace. This is to emerge finally—born again!

(25-2-51)

Many complain that they are unable in meditation successfully to bring their active thoughts to an end. In the ancient Indian art of yoga, this cessation—called nirvikalpa samadhi in Sanskrit—is placed as the highest stage to be reached by the practitioner. This situation must be viewed from two separate and distinct standpoints: from that of yoga and from that of philosophy. Would-be philosophers seek to become established in that insight into Reality which is called Truth. Intuitive feeling is a higher manifestation of man's faculties. So long as the feeling itself remains unobstructed by illusions, and—after incessant reflection, inquiry, study, remembrance, reverence, aspiration, training of thought, and purification—a man finds the insight dawning in his mind, he may not need to practise meditation. He may do so and he will feel the satisfaction and tranquillity which comes from it. Those who become sufficiently proficient in yoga, even if they achieve the complete cessation of thoughts, should still take up the pursuit of understanding and insight. If they are content with their attainment, they can remain for years enjoying the bliss, the tranquillity, the peace of a meditational state; but this does not mean knowledge in its fullest meaning.   (20-4-138)

Neither deep meditation nor the experience can give more than a temporary glimpse. The full and permanent enlightenment, which is to stay with a man and never leave him, can only come after he has clear insight into the nature of Overself.   (22-8-11)

In this astonishing revelation, he discovers that he himself is the seeker, the teacher, and the sought-for goal.   (28-2-153)

Is insight achieved gradually or suddenly, as the Zen Buddhists claim? Here again both claims are correct, if taken together as parts of a larger and fuller view. We have to begin by cultivating intuitive feelings. These come to us infrequently at first and so the process is a gradual and long one. Eventually, we reach a point, a very advanced point, where the ego sees its own limitation, perceives its helplessness and dependence, realizes that it cannot lift itself up into the final illuminations. It should then surrender itself wholly to the Overself and cast its further development on the mercy and Grace of the power beyond it. It will then have to go through a waiting period of seeming inactivity, spiritual stagnation, and inability to feel the fervour of devotion which it formerly felt. This is a kind of dark night of the soul. Then, slowly, it begins to come out of this phase, which is often accompanied by mental depression and emotional frustration into a higher phase where it feels utterly resigned to the will of God or destiny, calm and peaceful in the sense of accepting that higher will and not in any joyous sense, patiently waiting for the time when the infinite wisdom will bring it what it once sought so ardently but what it is now as detached from as it is detached from worldly ambitions. After this phase there will come suddenly unexpectedly and in the dead of night, as it were, a tremendous Realization of the egoless state, a tremendous feeling of liberation from itself as it has known itself, a tremendous awareness of the infinitude, universality, and intelligence of life. With that, new perceptions into the Laws of the cosmos will suddenly unfold themselves. The seeker must thus pass from intuition into insight.   (25-2-55)

To the man who has come along the path of loving devotion to God and finally gained the reward of frequent, joyous, ardent, inward communion with God, equally as to the man who has practised the way of mystical self-recollection and attained frequent awareness of the Overself's presence, an unexpected and unpalatable change may happen little by little or suddenly. God will seem to withdraw from the devotee, the Overself from the mystic. The blisses will fade and end. Although this experience will have none of the terror or isolation and misery of the "dark night" it will be comparable to that unforgettable time. And although it will seem like a withdrawal of Grace, the hidden truth is that it is actually a farther and deeper bestowal of Grace. For the man is being led to the next stage—which is to round out, balance, and complete his development. This he will be taught to do by first, acquiring cosmological knowledge, and later, attaining ontological wisdom. That is, he will learn something about the World-Idea and then, this gained, pass upward to learning the nature of that Reality in whose light even the universe is illusion. Thus from study of the operations of the Power behind the World-Idea he passes on to pondering on the Power itself. This last involves the highest degree of concentration and is indeed the mysterious little practised Yoga of the Uncontradictable. When successfully followed it brings about the attainment of Insight, the final discovery that there is no other being than THAT, no second entity.   (22-8-24)

Nirvikalpa/Void

This mysterious experience seems also to have been known to Dionysius the Areopagite. It is definitely an experience terminating the process of meditation, for the mystic can then go no higher and no deeper. It is variously called "the Nought" in the West and nirvikalpa samadhi in the East. Everything in the world vanishes and along with the world goes the personal ego; nothing indeed is left except Consciousness-in-Itself. If anything can burrow under the foundations of the ego and unsettle its present and future stability, it is this awesome event. But, because it is still an experience, it has a coming and a going. Although it is forever after remembered, a memory is not the final settled condition open to man—for that, philosophy must be brought in. Mysticism may remove the ego temporarily after first lulling it, but philosophy understands the ego, puts it in its place, its subservient place, so that the man remains always undeserted by the pure consciousness. (20-4-116)

Whoever succeeds in going down deeply enough into his own consciousness can find a phase where it passes away as person, as the limited little self, but is transformed into the Universal being and then, still farther, into the Void. This Void is not the annihilation of Consciousness but the fullness of it, not blankness but true awareness, unhindered by subsiding activities, not the adulteration of it by thoughts or imaginations but the purity of it. In this way he experiences his own personal self-nothingness. From this he can understand two things: why so many prophets have taught that self blocks our way and why the Mahayana Buddhists have taught the reality of the Void. (23-8-73)

There is, in this third stage, a condition that never fails to arouse the greatest wonder when initiation into it begins. In certain ways it corresponds to, and mentally parallels, the condition of the embryo in a mother's womb. Therefore, it is called by mystics who have experienced it "the second birth." The mind is drawn so deeply into itself and becomes so engrossed in itself that the outer world vanishes utterly. The sensation of being enclosed all round by a greater presence, at once protective and benevolent, is strong. There is a feeling of being completely at rest in this soothing presence. The breathing becomes very quiet and hardly perceptible. One is aware also that nourishment is being mysteriously and rhythmically drawn from the universal Life-force. Of course, there is no intellectual activity, no thinking, and no need of it. Instead, there is a k-n-o-w-i-n-g. There are no desires, no wishes, no wants. A happy peacefulness, almost verging on bliss, as human love might be without its passions and pettinesses, holds one in magical thrall. In its freedom from mental working and perturbation, from passional movement and emotional agitation, the condition bears something of infantile innocence. Hence Jesus' saying: "Except ye become as little children ye shall in no wise enter the Kingdom of Heaven." But essentially it is a return to a spiritual womb, to being born again into a new world of being where at the beginning he is personally as helpless, as weak, and as dependent as the physical embryo itself. (23-7-11)

Everything that intrudes upon the mental stillness in this highly critical stage must be rejected, no matter how virtuous or how "spiritual" a face it puts on. Only by the lapse of all thought, by the loss of all thinking capacity can he maintain this rigid stillness as it should be maintained. It is here alone that the last great battle will be fought and that the first great fulfilment will be achieved. That battle will be the one which will give the final deathblow to the ego; that fulfilment will be the union with his Overself after the ego's death. Both the battle and the fulfilment must take place within the stillness; they must not be a merely intellectual matter of thought alone nor a merely emotional matter of feeling alone. Here in the stillness both thought and emotion must die and the ego will then lose their powerful support. Therefore here alone is it possible to tackle the ego with any possibility of victory. (23-8-153)

When the personal ego's thoughts and desires are stripped off, we behold ourselves as we were in the first state and as we shall be in the final one. We are then the Overself alone, in its Godlike solitude and stillness. (24-4-1)

When he travels the course of meditation into the deep places of his being, and if he plumbs them to their utmost reach, at the end he crosses the threshold of the Void and enters a state which is nonbeing to the ego. For no memory and no activity of his personal self can exist there. Yet it is not annihilation, for one thing remains—Consciousness. In this way, and regarding what happens from the standpoint of his ordinary state at a later time, he learns that this residue is his real being, his very Spirit, his enduring life. He learns too why every movement which takes him out of the Void stillness into a personal mental activity is a return to an inferior state and a descent to a lower plane. He sees that among such movements there must necessarily be classed even the answering of such thoughts as "I am a Master. He is my disciple," or "I am being used to heal the disease of this man." In his own mind he is neither a teacher nor a healer. If other men choose to consider him as such and gain help toward sinlessness or get cured of sickness, he takes no credit to himself for the result but looks at it as if the "miracle" were done by a stranger. (23-8-71)

I remember the first time I had this astonishing experience. I was fond of disappearing from London whenever the weather allowed and wandering alongside the river Thames in its more picturesque country parts. If the day was sunny I would stretch my feet out, lie down in the grass, pull out notebook and pen from my pocket—knowing that thoughts would eventually arise that would have for me an instructive or even revelatory nature, apart from those ordinary ones which were merely expressive. One day, while I was waiting for these thoughts to arise, I lost the feeling that I was there at all. I seemed to dissolve and vanish from that place, but not from consciousness. Something was there, a presence, certainly not me, but I was fully aware of it. It seemed to be something of the highest importance, the only thing that mattered. After a few minutes I came back, discovered myself in time and space again; but a great peace had touched me and a very benevolent feeling was still with me. I looked at the trees, the shrubs, the flowers, and the grass and felt a tremendous sympathy with them and then when I thought of other persons a tremendous benevolence towards them. (22-6-80)

The actual experience alone can settle this argument. This is what I found: The ego vanished; the everyday "I" which the world knew and which knew the world, was no longer there. But a new and diviner individuality appeared in its place, a consciousness which could say "I AM" and which I recognized to have been my real self all along. It was not lost, merged, or dissolved: it was fully and vividly conscious that it was a point in universal Mind and so not apart from that Mind itself. Only the lower self, the false self, was gone but that was a loss for which to be immeasurably grateful. (28-2-142)

The ego totally ceases to exist and is fully absorbed into the Overself only in special, temporary, and trance-like states. At all other times, and certainly at all ordinary active and everyday times, it continues to exist. The failure to learn and understand this important point always causes much confusion in mystical circles. The state arrived at in deep meditation is one thing; the state returned to after such meditation is another. The ego vanishes in one but reappears in the other. But there are certain after-effects of this experience upon it which bring about by degrees a shift in its relation to the Overself. It submits, obeys, expresses, and reflects the Overself. (8-1-213)

In deepest contemplation, the Nirvikalpa Samadhi of the Indian yogis, both egolessness and blissful peace can be experienced. But it is a temporary state; return to the world must follow, so the quest is not finished. The next step or stage is *application*, putting into the active everyday life this egoless detachment and this satisfying calmness.   (24-3-319)

The world abruptly vanishes from his ken. He is poised for a few minutes in No-thing, the same great Void in which God is eternally poised. His contemplation has succeeded and, succeeding, has led him from self to Overself.   (23-8-94)

If there is no such entity as a "me," an ego, you are entitled to ask *who* then has this enlightenment? And the answer is the only possible one: it is the Void having the experience of itself: or rediscovering itself as it does in each person who attains this level.   (25-2-221)

He who passes through these deeper phases of the Void can never again call anything or anyone his own. He becomes secretly and spiritually deprived of all personal possessions. This is because he has thoroughly realized the complete immateriality, spacelessness, timelessness, and formlessness of the Real—a realization which consequently leaves him nothing to take hold of, either within the world or within his personality. Not only does the possessive sense fall away from his attitude towards physical things but also towards intellectual ones.   (23-8-180)

Our thoughts pass out and evaporate into a seeming void. Can it be that this void is really a nothingness, really less existent than the thoughts it receives? No, the void is nothing other, can be nothing other than Mind itself. The thoughts merge inward in their secret essence—Thought.   (19-5-15)

Psychologically the void trance is deeper than the world-knowing insight, but metaphysically it is not. For in both cases one and the same Reality is seen.   (23-7-301)

The Infinite cannot be set against the finite as though they were a pair of opposites. Only things which are on the same level can be opposed to one another. These are not. The Infinite includes and contains within itself all possible finites. The practical import of this truth is that Mind cannot only be experienced in the Void but also in the world. The Reality is not only to be discovered as it is but also beneath its phenomenal disguises.   (20-4-124)

Yet the deeper we travel, the less need have we of thoughts and words, for all multiplicity collapses in this marvelous unity. We can neither think nor talk of this sublime state with any accuracy. Hence the only medium whereby we can properly represent it is—silence!   (1-6-778)

Sahaja

The general idea in the popular and religious circles of India is that the highest state of illumination is attained during a trance condition (samadhi). This is not the teaching in the highest philosophic circles of India. There is another condition, *sahaja samadhi*, which is described in a few little-known texts and which is regarded as superior. It is esteemed because no trance is necessary and because it is a continuous state. The inferior state is one which is intermittently entered and left: it cannot be retained without returning to trance. The philosophic "fourth state," by contrast, remains unbroken even when active and awake in the busy world. (25-2-147)

What is the difference between the state of deepest contemplation, which the Hindus call nirvikalpa samadhi, and that which they call sahaja samadhi? The first is only a temporary experience, that is it begins and ends but the man actually experiences an uplift of consciousness, he gains a new and higher outlook. But sahaja is continuous unbroken realization that as Overself he always was, is, and shall be. It is not a feeling that something new and higher has been gained. What is the absolute test which distinguishes one condition from the other, since both are awareness of the Overself? In nirvikalpa the ego vanishes but reappears when the ordinary state is resumed: hence it has only been lulled, even though it has been slightly weakened by the process. In sahaja the ego is rooted out once and for all! It not only vanishes, but it cannot reappear. (25-2-139)

The Overself should not be reached merely in trance; it must be known in full waking consciousness. Trance is merely the deepest phase of meditation, which in turn is instrumental in helping prepare the mind to discover truth. Yoga does not yield truth directly. Trance does not do more than concentrate the mind perfectly and render it completely calm. Realization can come after the mind is in that state and after it has begun to inquire, with such an improved instrument, into truth. (23-7-122)

It must be remembered that the glimpse is not the goal of life. It is a happening, something which begins and ends, but something which is of immense value in contributing to the philosophic life, its day-to-day consciousness, its ordinary stabilized nature.

Philosophic life is established continuously and permanently in the divine presence; the glimpse comes and goes within that presence. The glimpse is exceptional and exciting; but sahaja, the established state, is ordinary, normal, every day. The glimpse tends to withdraw us from activity, even if only for a few moments, whereas sahaja does not have to stop its outward activity.

(22-8-23)

Ramana Maharshi often used the term sahaja samadhi to describe what he regarded as the best state. Although the word samadhi is too often associated with yogic trance, there is nothing of the kind in his use of this term. He said it was the best state because it was quite natural, nothing forced, artificial, or temporary. We may equate it with Zen's "This life is very life" and "Walk On!"

(25-2-133)

It is the art of being artless, spiritual without doing it consciously. It is achievement of effortless mental quiet. It is ordinary living, plus an extraordinary continuous awareness.   (23-1-142)

I am an Advaitin on the fundamental point of nonduality of the Real, but I am unable to limit myself to most Advaitin's practical view of samadhi and sahaja. Here I stand with Chinese Zen (Ch'an), especially as I was taught and as explained by the Sixth Patriarch, Hui Neng. He warns against turning meditation into a narcotic, resulting in a pleasant passivity. He went so far as to declare: "It is quite unnecessary to stay in monasteries. Only let your mind . . . function in freedom . . . let it abide nowhere." And in this connection he later explains: "To be free from attachment to all outer objects is true meditation. To meditate means to realize thus tranquillity of Essence of Mind."

On samadhi, he defines it as a mind self-trained to be

unattached amid objects, resting in tranquillity and peace. On sahaja, it is thorough understanding of the truth about reality and a penetration into and through delusion, to one's Essence of Mind. The Indian notion of sahaja makes it the extension of nirvikalpa samadhi into the active everyday state. But the Ch'an conception of nirvikalpa samadhi differs from this; it does not seek deliberately to eliminate thoughts, although that may often happen of its own accord through identification with the true Mind, but to eliminate the personal feelings usually attached to them, that is, to remain unaffected by them because of this identification.

Ch'an does not consider sahaja to be the fruit of yoga meditation alone, nor of understanding alone, but of a combination seemingly of both. It is a union of reason and intuition. It is an awakening once and for all. It is not attained in nirvikalpa and then to be held as long as possible. It is not something, a state alternately gained and lost on numerous occasions, but gradually expanded as it is clung to. It is a single awakening that enlightens the man so that he never returns to ignorance again. He has awakened to his divine essence, his source in Mind, as an all day and every day self-identification. It has come by itself, effortlessly.

(25-2-141)

Were the glorious realization of the Overself devoid of any feeling, then the realization itself would be a palpable absurdity. It would not be worth having. The grand insight into reality is certainly not stripped of fervent delight and is surely not an arid intellectual concept. It is rightly saturated with exalted emotion but it is not this emotion alone. The beatific feeling of what is real is quite compatible with precise knowledge of what is real; there is no contradiction between them. Indeed they must coexist. Nay, there is a point on the philosophic path where they even run into each other. Such a point marks the beginning of a stable wisdom which will not be the victim of merciless alternation between the ebb and the flow of a rapturous emotionalism but will know that it dwells in timelessness here and now; therefore it will not be subject to such fluctuations of mood. Better than the exuberant upsurges and emotional depressions of the mystical temperament is the mental evenness which is without rise or fall and which should be the aim of the far-seeing students. The fitful flashes of enlightenment pertaining to the mystic stage are replaced by a steady light only when the philosophic stage is reached and passed through. The philosophic aim is to overcome the difference between sporadic intuitions and steady knowledge, between spasmodic ecstasies and controlled perception, and thus achieve a permanent state of enlightenment, abiding unshakeably and at all times in the Overself. (20-4-22)

When you awaken to truth as it really is, you will have no occult vision, you will have no "astral" experience, no ravishing ecstasy. You will awaken to it in a state of utter stillness, and you will realize that truth was *always* there within you and that reality was always there around you. Truth is not something which has grown and developed through your efforts. It is not something which has been achieved or attained by laboriously adding up those efforts. It is not something which has to be made more and more perfect each year. And once your mental eyes are opened to truth they can never be closed again. (25-2-77)

Sahaja samadhi is not broken into intervals, is permanent, and involves no special effort. Its arisal is instantaneous and without progressive stages. It can accompany daily activity without interfering with it. It is a settled calm and complete inner quiet. There are no distinguishing marks that an outside observer can use to identify a sahaja-conscious man because sahaja represents consciousness itself rather than its transitory states.

Sahaja has been called the lightning flash. Philosophy considers it to be the most desirable goal.

This is illustrated with a classic instance of Indian spirituality involving a king named Janaka. One day he was about to mount his horse and put one foot into the stirrup which hung from the saddle. As he was about to lift himself upwards into the saddle the "lightning flash" struck his consciousness. He was instantly carried away and concentrated so deeply that he failed for some time to lift himself up any higher. From that day onwards he lived in sahaja samadhi which was always present within him.

Those at the state of achieved sahaja are under no compulsion to continue to meditate any more or to practise yoga. They often do—either because of inclinations produced by past habits or as a means of helping other persons. In either case it is experienced as a pleasure. Because this consciousness is permanent, the experiencer does not need to go into meditation. This is despite the outward appearance of a person who places himself in the posture of meditation in order to achieve something.

When you are engaged in outward activity it is not the same as when you are in a trance. This is true for both the beginner and the adept. The adept, however, does not lose the sahaja awareness which he has achieved and can withdraw into the depths of consciousness which the ordinary cannot do.   (25-2-138)

He who can stay in the world and keep his calmness in all conditions—whether they are attractive or repulsive—who can move in society without falling victim to the desires, attachments, or greeds which afflict it, who never lets go of the still divine centre within himself whether alone and quiet or with others and active, he is the real yogi and is experiencing the true samadhi.   (24-3-325)

Stages of Realization

The Witness is both an abstract metaphysical concept and a concrete mystical experience. It is not an ultimate one, yielding pure Being, the unsplit Consciousness, but a provisional one.

(25-2-98)

Although the aspirant has now awakened to his witness-self, found his "soul," and thus lifted himself far above the mass of mankind, he has not yet accomplished the full task set him by life. A further effort still awaits his hand. He has yet to realize that the witness-self is only a *part* of the All-self. So his next task is to discover that he is not merely the witness of the rest of existence but essentially of one stuff with it. He has, in short, by further meditations to realize his oneness with the entire universe in its real being. He must now meditate on his witness-self as being in its essence the infinite All. Thus the ultramystic exercises are graded into two stages, the second being more advanced than the first. The banishment of thoughts reveals the inner self whereas the reinstatement of thoughts without losing the newly gained consciousness reveals the All-inclusive universal self. The second feat is the harder.

(23-6-88)

He is not separate from his own experience, not an observer watching it. For there is only the inner silence, with which he is identified if he turns to examine the I, only the pure consciousness.

(22-3-294)

The translation of the Sanskrit phrase *antardrishti* is literally "inward seeing" in the sense of seeing beneath appearances what is under them. It does not refer to clairvoyance in the psychic sense, but rather to the metaphysical or mystical sense. It can be particularized as meaning entering into the witness state of consciousness. The ordinary person sees only the object; penetrating deeper, he enters the witness state which is an intermediate condition; going still deeper, he reaches the ultimate state of Reality when there is no subject or object, whereas in the witness there is still subject and object, but the subject no longer identifies himself with the object as the ordinary man does.   (22-8-85)

There are two paths laid out for the attainment, according to the teaching of Sri Krishna in the *Bhagavad Gita*. The first path is union with the Higher Self—not, as some believe, with the Logos. But because the Higher Self is a ray from the Logos, it is as near as a human being can get to it anyway. The second path has its ultimate goal in the Absolute, or as I have named it in my last book, the Great Void. But neither path contradicts the other, for the way to the second path lies through the first one. Therefore, there is no cleavage in the practices. Both goals are equally desirable because both bring man into touch with Reality. It would be quite proper for anyone to stop with the first one if he wishes; but for those who appreciate the philosophic point of view, the second goal, because it includes the first, is more desirable.

(1-5-115)

The momentary glimpse of the true self is not the ultimate experience. There is another yet more wonderful lying ahead. In this he will be bound by invisible hoops of wide selfless compassion to all living creatures. The detachment will be sublimated, taken up into a higher level, where the universal Unity will be truly felt.   (excerpted from 22-8-107)

Islamic mystics called Sufis differentiate between glimpses, which they call "states," and permanent advances on the path, which they call "stations." The former are described as being not only temporary but also fragmentary, while the latter are described as bearing results which cannot be lost. There are three main stations along the path. The first is annihilation of the ego; the second is rebirth in the Overself; and the third is fully grown union with the Overself. The Sufis assert that this final state can never be reached without the Grace of the Higher Power and that it is complete, lasting, and unchangeable. (22-8-28)

For us who are philosophically minded, the World-Mind truly exists. For us it is God, and for us there is a relationship with it—the relationship of devotion and aspiration, of communion and meditation. All the abstract talk about nonduality may go on, but in the end the talkers must humble themselves before the infinite Being until they are as nothing and until they are lost in the stillness—Its stillness. (27-1-72)

Fruits of the Path

What Is a Philosopher/Sage?

He is a man whose perception goes farther, whose awareness goes deeper than the rest of his fellow men. It must go so far and so deep that it rests durably in the "I Am" of the Overself. Without this he does not possess the first, the most essential and most important of all the credentials needed for communicating to others the art of attaining the Overself. The second credential, and admittedly a lesser one, is the compassionate desire to effect this communication as much as possible. The third is that he have special power to teach others what he knows.   (1-6-396)

The true philosopher is conscious daily of the blessed inward life of the Overself, indescribable in its serenity, loveliness, strength, and sacredness. Keeping the mind in equilibrium, in a state of equipoise which remains undistracted and undisturbed by external forces and events, becomes perfectly natural in time, and is a state in which he continues until death. It is not a monotonous condition as some might believe, but one of such satisfaction that we can only faintly envisage it in comparison with our material joys deprived of their emotional excitements.   (20-5-29)

Without keeping steadily in view this original mentalness of things and hence their original oneness with self and Mind, the mystic must naturally get confused if not deceived by what he takes to be the opposition of Spirit and Matter. The mystic looks within, to self; the materialist looks without, to world. And each *misses* what the other finds. But to the philosopher neither of these is primary. He looks to that Mind of which both self and world are but manifestations and in which he finds the manifestations also. It is not enough for him to receive, as the mystic receives, fitful and occasional illuminations from periodic meditation. He relates this intellectual understanding to his further discovery got during mystical self-absorption in the Void that the reality of his own self is Mind. Back in the world once more he studies it again under this further light, confirms that the manifold world consists ultimately of mental images, conjoins with his full meta-physical understanding that it is simply Mind in manifestation, and thus comes to comprehend that it is essentially one with the same Mind which he experiences in self-absorption. Thus his insight actualizes, experiences, this Mind-in-itself as and not apart from the sensuous world whereas the mystic divides them. With insight, the sense of oneness does not destroy the sense of difference but both remain strangely present, whereas with the ordinary mystical perception each cancels the other. The myriad forms which make up the picture of this world will not disappear as an essential characteristic of reality nor will his awareness of them or his traffic with them be affected. Hence he possesses a firm and final attainment wherein he will permanently possess the insight into pure Mind even in the midst of physical sensations. He sees everything in this multitudinous world as being but the Mind itself as easily as he can see nothing, the imageless Void, as being but the Mind itself, whenever he cares to turn aside into self-absorption. He sees both the outer faces of all men and the inner depths of his own self as being but the Mind itself. Thus he experiences the unity of all existence; not intermittently but at every moment he knows the Mind as ultimate. This is the philosophic or final realization. It is as permanent as the mystic's is transient. Whatever he does or refrains from doing, whatever he experiences or fails to experience, he gives up all discriminations between reality and appearance, between truth and illusion, and lets his insight function freely as his thoughts select and cling to nothing. He experiences the miracle of undifferentiated being, the wonder of undifferenced unity. The artificial man-made frontiers melt away. He sees his fellow men as inescapably and inherently divine as they are, not merely as the mundane creatures they believe they are, so that any traces of an ascetical holier-than-thou attitude fall completely away from him.   (28-2-154)

He is a philosopher who realizes to the full, and continually feels, the presence of divinity not only within himself but also within the world.   (20-5-30)

His relationship to the Overself is one of direct awareness of its presence—not as a separate being but as his own essence.

(25-2-301)

It is to live realization *while* behaving in the perfectly natural human way, and it is in this last sense that an old Oriental text describes the sage as bearing no distinguishing marks upon his person.   (25-3-378)

The discovery of his true being is not outwardly dramatic, and for a long time no one may know of it, except himself. The world may not honour him for it: he may die as obscure as he lived. But the purpose of his life has been fulfilled; and God's will has been done.   (25-2-78)

Just as a man who has escaped from the inside of a burning house and finds himself in the cool outdoors understands that he has attained safety, so the man who has escaped from greed, lust, anger, illusion, selfishness, and ignorance into exalted peace and immediate insight, understands that he has attained heaven.

(24-4-150)

Pain and suffering, sin and evil, disease and death, exist only in the world of thoughts, not in the world of pure Thought itself. They are not illusions, however, but they are transient. Whoever attains to pure Thought will also attain *in consciousness* to a life that is painless, sorrow-free, sinless, undecaying, and undying. Being above desires and fears, it is necessarily above the miseries caused by unsatisfied desires and realized fears. But at the same time he will also have an *accompanying* consciousness of life in the body, which must obey the laws of its own being, natural laws which set limitations and imperfections upon it.   (10-1-78)

The effects of enlightenment include: an imperturbable detachment from outer possessions, rank, honours, and persons; an overwhelming certainty about truth; a carefree, heavenly peace above all disturbances and vicissitudes; an acceptance of the general rightness of the universal situation, with each entity and each event playing its role; and impeccable sincerity which says what it means, means what it says.   (25-2-255)

Of little use are explanations which befog truth and bewilder understanding. To inform a Western reader that an enlightened man sees only "Brahman" is to imply that he does not see forms, that is, the world. But the fact is that he *does* see what unenlightened men see—the physical objects and creatures around him—or he could not attend to the simplest little necessity or duty of which all humans have to take care. But he sees things without being limited to their physical appearance—he knows their inner reality too. (25-2-243)

It is not only possible to attain these brief glimpses of the Overself, but also to attain a durable lasting consciousness of it. No change of this state can then happen. The adept discovers that its future is no different from but quite the same as its past. This is the sacred Eternal Now. Only by this abiding light is it possible to see how mixed and imperfect are all earlier and transient experiences. (22-8-12)

The mystic will not care and may not be able to do so but the philosopher has to learn the art of combining his inward recognition of the Void with his outward activity amongst things without feeling the slightest conflict between both. Such an art is admittedly difficult but it can be learnt with time and patience and comprehension. Thus he will feel inward unity everywhere in this world of wonderful variety, just as he will experience all the countless mutations of experience as being present in the very midst of this unity. (20-4-121)

There are no breaks in the awareness of his higher nature. There is no loss of continuity in the consciousness of his immortal spirit. Therefore he is not illumined at some hour of the day and unillumined at another hour, nor illumined while he is awake and unillumined while he is asleep. (25-2-178)

The sage does not retire at night in the darkness, the ignorance of ordinary sleep, but in the light of the Consciousness, the ever-unbroken Transcendence. (25-2-176)

There will be a zone of peace around him which some feel but others cannot. It seems to put him quite at his ease and free him from any trace of nervousness. (24-4-105)

The Master *has* found his way to the Overself; he daily enjoys the blessing of its presence; he has passed from mere existence into significant living, and he knows there is peace and love at the heart of the universe. He wants now to help others share in the fruits of his discoveries. (25-6-22)

Despite popular superstition and wishful thinking it is true that no master can bestow his own enlightenment on others as a permanent gift. But does this make his attainment valueless to them? No, for it proves to them both that the Overself *is* and that man may commune with it. The few who are more sensitive or more perceptive gain more from personal contact with him—either inspiration for their quest or, if more fortunate, a momentary glimpse of the far-off goal. (1-6-836)

The illuminate is conscious both of the ultimate unity and immediate multiplicity of the world. This is a paradox. But his permanent resting place while he is dealing with others is at the junction-point of duality and unity so that he is ready at any moment to absorb his attention in either phase. (25-2-115)

This is the true insight, the permanent illumination that neither comes nor goes but always *is*. While being serious, where the event or situation requires it, he will not be solemn. For behind this seriousness there is detachment. He cannot take the world of Appearances as being Reality's final form. If he is a sharer in this world's experiences, he is also a witness and especially a witness of his own ego—its acts and desires, its thoughts and speech. And because he sees its littleness, he keeps his sense of humour about all things concerning it, a touch of lightness, a basic humility. Others may believe that he stands in the Great Light, but he himself has no particular or ponderous self-importance.   (20-4-205)

Individuality of the Sage

God is never identified with any man, nor incarnated in him. For God alone is uniquely the Unindividuated whereas all men are individualized creatures. Even the highest type of man, the sage-saviour, is a particular light, whereas God is the light itself.   (25-1-170)

There is much confusion of understanding about what happens to the ego when it attains the ultimate goal. Some believe that a cosmic consciousness develops, with an all-knowing intelligence and an "all-overish" feeling. They regard it as unity with the whole universe. Others assert that there is a complete loss of the ego, an utter destruction of the personal self. No—these are confused notions of what actually occurs. The Overself is not a collective entity as though it were composed of a number of particles. One's embrace of other human beings through it is not in union with them but only in sympathy, not in psychic identification with them but in psychic harmony. He has enlarged the area of his vision and sees himself as a part of mankind. But this does not mean that he has become conscious of all mankind as though they were himself. The true unity is with one's own higher indestructible self. It is still with a higher individuality, not a cosmic one, and it is still with one's own self, not with the rest of mankind. Unity with them is neither mystically nor practically possible. What we discover is discovered by a deepening of consciousness, not by a widening of it. Hence it is not so much a wider as a deeper self that he has first to find.

With the rectification of this error, we may find the correct answer to the question: "What is the practical meaning of the injunction laid by all the great spiritual teachers upon their followers, to give up the ego, to renounce the self?" It does not ask for a foolish sentimentality, in the sense that we are to be as putty in the hands of all other men. It does not ask for an utter impossibility, in the sense that we are never to attend to our own affairs at all. It does not ask for a useless absurdity, in the sense that we are to become oblivious of our very existence. On the contrary, it asks for what is wise, practicable, and worthwhile—that we give up our lower personality to our higher individuality.

Thus it is not that the aspirant is asked to abandon all thought of his particular self (as if he could) or to lose consciousness of it, but that he is asked to perceive its imperfection, its unsatisfactoriness, its faultiness, its baseness and its sinfulness and, in consequence of this perception, to give it up in favour of his higher self, with its perfection, blessedness, goodness, nobility, and wisdom. For in the lower ego he will never know peace whereas in the diviner one he will always know it.   (22-3-108)

Is the ego totally lost, utterly obliterated in this attainment? I can only say that none of our usual concepts fit the actual result, that it is hard to describe, and that suggestion must here replace description. For the ego and the Overself fuse and unite, yet the union does not destroy the ego's capacity to express itself or to be active in the world. Its own annihilation is a transient experience during the contemplative state. Its resumption of worldly life while permanently established in perfect harmony with, and obedience to, the divine Overself is the further and final goal.

(8-1-207)

When it is said that we lose our individuality on entering Nirvana, words are being used loosely and faultily. So long as a man, whether he be Buddha or Hitler, has to walk, eat, and work, he must use his individuality. What *is* lost by the sage is his *attachment* to individuality with its desires, hates, angers, and passions.

(25-2-190)

When he has silenced his desires and stilled his thoughts, when he has put his own will aside and his own ego down, he becomes a free channel through which the Divine Mind may flow into his own consciousness. No evil feelings can enter his heart, no evil thoughts can cross his mind, and not even the new consequence of old wrong-doing can affect his serenity.   (20-5-48)

Despite all the high idealistic talk of oneness, brotherhood and egolessness, each of us is still an individual, still has to dwell in a body of his own, to use a mind of his own and experience feelings of his own. To forget this is to practise self-deception. Each will come to God in the end but he will come as a purified transformed and utterly changed person, lived in and used by God as he himself will live in and be conscious of the presence of God.   (1-3-97)

The differences between human beings still remain after illumination. The variations which make each one a unique specimen and the individual that he is, still continue to exist. But the Oneness behind human beings powerfully counterbalances.   (25-2-189)

For the man in that high consciousness and identified with it, the ego is simply an open channel through which his being may flow into the world of time and space. It is not himself, as it is for the unenlightened man, but an adjunct to himself, obeying and expressing his will. (8-1-210)

Give the ego back to the Overself and then the Overself will use it as it should be used—in harmony with the cosmic laws of being. This means that the welfare of all others in contact with the ego will be considered as well as the ego's own. (22-2-49)

Sage's Knowledge

From that moment when he understands human problems with the wisdom of the Overself, his thinking will become illumined from within, as it were. He will comprehend clearly the inner significance of each problem that presents itself. (20-5-19)

One of the foremost features of enlightenment is the clarity it gives to the mind, the lucidity of understanding and luminosity which surrounds all problems. (25-2-277)

He will look at experience from a new centre. He will see all things and creatures not only as they are on earth but also as they are "in heaven." (20-5-114)

He does not claim to be a walking encyclopaedia nor ask for a halo of infallibility. There are many questions to which he does not know the true answers. He is neither pontifically infallible nor deifically omniscient. What the philosophical teacher seeks to establish are the basic principles in which all true seeking must end. (20-4-291)

There is some confusion on this point in the minds of many students. On attaining enlightenment a man does not attain omniscience. At most, he may receive a revelation of the inner operations of life and Nature, of the higher laws governing life and man. That is, he may also become a seer and find a cosmogony presented to his gaze. But the actuality in a majority of cases is that he attains enlightenment only, not cosmogonical seership.

(25-2-108)

When a man has reached this stage, where his will and life are surrendered and his mind and heart are aware of divine presences, he learns that it is practical wisdom not to decide his future in advance but rather to let it grow out of itself like corn out of seed. (18-4-188)

When we come at last to perceive that all this vast universe is a thought-form and when we can feel our own source to be the single and supreme principle in and through which it arises, then our knowledge has become final and perfect. (21-5-178)

Sage's Compassion

It is a state of exquisite tenderness, of love welling up from an inner centre and radiating outward in all directions. If other human beings or animal creatures come within his contact at the time, they become recipients of this love without exception. For then no enemies are recognized, none are disliked, and it is not possible to regard anyone as repulsive. (22-6-83)

One fruit of the change will be that just as the old idea was to watch out selfishly for his own interests, so the new idea will be not to separate them from the interests of others. If it be asked, "How can anyone who is attuned to such impersonality be also benevolent?" the answer is that because he is also attuned to the real Giver of all things, he need not struggle against anyone nor possess anything. Hence he can afford to be generous as the selfish cannot. And because the Overself's very nature is harmony and love, he seeks the welfare of others alongside of his own.   (6-1-387)

The state of nonduality is a state of intense peace and perfect balance. It is so peaceful because everything is seen as it belongs—to the eternal order of cosmic evolution; hence, all is accepted, all reconciled.   (25-2-124)

Whosoever enters into this realization becomes a human sun who sheds enlightenment, radiates strength, and emanates love to all beings.   (25-3-146)

If he keeps in right relation with his Overself, he will inevitably keep in right relation with everything and everyone else. (23-1-174)

He takes people just as he finds them and events just as they happen. He does not outwardly express any desire for them to be different from what they are. There are at least two reasons for this attitude. First, he knows that the divine thought of the universe contains the idea of evolution. So he believes that however bad people may be, one day they will be better; however untoward circumstances may be, divine wisdom has brought them about. Second, he knows that if he is to keep an unruffled peace inside him, he must allow nothing outside him to disturb it. Because he regards the outer life as being as ephemeral as a dream, he is reconciled to everything, rebellious against nothing.   (20-5-115)

The sage can condemn nobody, can regard none as outside his range of compassion, and can find a place in his heart for the worst sinner. He knows that duality is but a dream and discovers himself anew in all sentient creatures. He knows that the world's woe arises out of its false and fictitious sense of separateness.

(25-3-288)

The sage has conquered separativeness in his mind and realized the ALL as himself. The logical consequence is tremendous. It follows that there is no liberation from the round of births and rebirths for the sage; he has to go through it like the others. Of course, he does this with full understanding whereas they are plunged in darkness. But if he identifies himself with the All, then he can't desert but must go on to the end, working for the liberation of others in turn. This is his crucifixion, that being able to save others he is unable to save himself. "And the scripture was fulfilled, which saith, `And he was numbered with the transgressors.'" Why? Because compassion rules him, not the ego. Nobody is likely to want such a goal (until, indeed he is almost ready for it) so it is usually kept secret or symbolized. Again: "For this is my blood of the new testament, which is shed for many for the remission of sins."

(25-4-42)

Sage's Action

He gives each moment the best that is in him, and so living from moment to moment becomes a glorious adventure.

(23-5-211)

"In carrying water and chopping wood—there is the wonderful Tao." This ancient Chinese sentence is a subtle, clever way of saying that not only in meditation is the glimpse to be sought, but also in the world's work and life it is to be found and kept. Such is the ultimate state, this emptiness of mind amid activity of body. It is possible only by knowledge, the unforgettable recognition and understanding that within this emptiness lies Tao.

(22-8-84)

He understands then what it means to do nothing of himself, for he feels clearly that the higher power is doing through him whatever has to be done, is doing it rightly, while he himself is merely watching what is happening. (25-2-257)

His behaviour is spontaneous, but not through mere impulse nor through unused intellect. It is the spontaneity, the forthrightness of an inspired man who knows where he is going and what he is doing, who is directly guided in his relations with other men by a higher will than his own ego's. (22-2-51)

He who knows and feels the divine power in his inmost being will be set free in the most literal sense of the word from anxieties and cares. He who has not yet arrived at this stage but is on the way to it can approach the same desirable result by the intensity of his faith in that being. But such a one must really have the faith and not merely say so. The proof that he possesses it would lie in the measure with which he refuses to accept negative thoughts, fearful thoughts, despondent thoughts. In the measure that he does not fail in his faith and hence in his thinking, in that measure, the higher power will not fail to support him in his hour of need. This is why Jesus told his disciples, "Take no anxious thought for the morrow." In the case of the adept, having given up the ego, there is no one left to take care of him, so the higher Self does so for him. In the case of the believer, although he has not yet given up the ego, nevertheless, he is trying to do so, and his unfaltering trust in the higher Self is rewarded proportionately in the same way. In both cases the biblical phrase, "The Lord will provide," is not merely a pious hope but a practical fact. (20-3-97)

If he has really turned his life over to the higher power, then he need not crease his brow trying to work out his own plans.

He can wait either for the inner urge to direct him or for new circumstances to guide his actions.   (18-4-173)

The actions of a man who has attained this degree are inspired directly by his Overself, and consequently are not dictated by personal wishes, purposes, passions, or desires. They are not initiated by his ego's will but by a will higher than his own.

Since there is no consciously deliberate thinking, no attempt at ordered logical formulation of ideas, there is also no hesitation, no broken trends. There is only spontaneous thought, feeling, and action, all being directed by intuition   (25-2-88)

Whoever acts by becoming so pliable as to let the Overself hold his personal will, must necessarily become inwardly detached from the personal consequences of his deeds. This will be true whether those consequences be pleasant or unpleasant. Such detachment liberates him from the power of karma, which can no longer catch him in its web, for "he" is not there. His emotional consciousness preceding an action is always enlightened and characterized by sublime composure, whereas the unenlightened man's may be characterized by motivations of self-centered desire, ambition, fear, hope, greed, passion, dislike, or even hate—all of which are karma-making.   (24-3-280)

There is no single pattern that an intuitively guided life must follow. Sometimes he will see in a flash of insight both course and destination, but at other times he will see only the next step ahead and will have to keep an open mind both as to the second step and as to the final destination.   (22-1-261)

What he has to do in the world as a human being is henceforth to be done not really by his ordinary personal self but by the Presence which, shapeless and silent though it be, is the vital living essence of what connects him with God. If this seems to deprive him of the attributes which make a man *man*, I can reply only that we are here back with the Sphinx. Yes, the enigma is great; but the realized understanding and experience is immeasurably greater in its blessedness. (25-2-206)

When the ego is displaced and the Overself is using him, there will be no need and no freedom to choose between two alternatives in regard to actions. Only a single course will present itself, directly and unwaveringly, as the right one. (22-2-53)

Ad Infinitum

His quest *for* God has reached its terminus but his quest *in* God will now start its course. Henceforth his life, experience, and consciousness are wrapped in mystery.   (23-4-54)

The Long and Short Paths

As dictated by Paul Brunton to
Jeff Cox during a 1975 visit

ONE AFTERNOON Paul Brunton and I were sitting in his colorful living room in Switzerland chatting about various topics. After what seemed like a long pause in the conversation, he asked me if I knew about the Short Path to enlightenment. Up to that time, I had become very familiar with the path of purification and trying to understand the teachings, but I had not heard that there was a shorter way to accomplish the much-needed personal transformation. As he began to describe the Short Path, I quickly gathered my pencil and notebook and wrote as he spoke the following teaching.

Before, in the books, PB had to introduce people to the Quest and the preparations for the two paths—now we are ready to hear about the two paths—the long and the short.

St. Bernard expressed the long path thus:

Despise the world—(for it is unsatisfactory)

Despise yourself—(for it is also unsatisfactory)

Despise yourself because you despise yourself—
   (for even to despise yourself is to give the ego undue
   attention and concern).

This is the end of the long path. At this point one must turn around to the positive way which is the short path:

Glorify the world—(for it is an emanation of Brahman)

Glorify yourSelf

Glorify yourself because you glorify yourSelf

Rather than concerning oneself with the ego and its developments, its ups and downs, you should turn 180 degrees around and face the sun which is the Overself. The ego is like a whirlpool, a vortex of thoughts, and it is the strength of our clinging that holds it together. The ego is perpetuated on the long path which will not take you to enlightenment. On the long path you are always measuring your own progress. The long path is endless for new circumstances bring new temptations, new problems to deal with, and no matter how spiritual the ego becomes it does not enter the light but remains in the grey. On the long path the surges of interference arising from the lower self and the negativity which enters from the environment must be dealt with. This requires development of character.

On the short path one ignores negativity, and turns 180 degrees away from the ego to the Overself—things will become brighter and brighter. The short path will establish you in peace more and more. The work of the long path eventually brings the grace which then puts you on the short path. The short path is shorter in time for you turn and face your goal directly. Because of the pressures of these times, it is recommended that both paths be done together (rather than just the long) in order to help circumvent obstacles.

The parable of the cave in Plato is analogous to the short and long path. On the long path you back out of the cave but continue to look into the cave, into the darkness of the ego. On the short path you walk forwards toward the opening of the cave where the light is, the Overself.

There are two exercises suggested for the short path, one called the remembrance exercise, and the other, the "As If" exercise. The short path begins with the effort of remembering the Overself. The remembrance exercise overlaps the "As If" exercise and is a necessary preparatory exercise before the "As If" can be learned. The remembrance exercise is mentioned near the end of *The Wisdom of the Overself*. It is like a mother who has lost her baby and no matter what she is doing she can't forget about the child. When you are active the remembrance should be held in the rear of the mind, and when you have free time, it should come to the fore. In the beginning, it requires effort like any other practice, but eventually it will continue of its own accord. One danger of the remembrance exercise is that it can become automatic too soon and thus be merely mechanical and hollow. The remembrance must be a warm, felt, living thing if the spirit of the exercise is not to be lost. By turning towards the Overself, grace can operate more readily in all matters.

The "As If" exercise requires that one should feel and act and think everything as you imagine the Overself would. It is not just a mental exercise but involves the feeling, physical activity, and imagination. The Overself contacts you primarily through intuitive feeling but also through intuitive thoughts and action. Actions which are done uncalculatingly and which later prove to have been correct are actions which spring from a source other than the ego. In the beginning, the exercise is an imaginative one, but every so often one will get short glimpses which will gradually be prolonged and which are not imaginative but the real thing. As these glimpses of the Overself come, one must open up to them, be passive and receptive to them, you must surrender yourself to them and prolong them. This exercise should be accompanied with study of the nature of the Overself—so that you can know something of what the Overself is like and what it is that you are trying to do. However, the Overself is truly ineffable and can never be grasped through any secondary means.

Glossary

Advaita Vedanta: Appreciation of the teachings of Hinduism and its highest expression, the Advaita, is increasing in the West. And, thanks to T.M.P. Mahadevan, His Holiness' [Shankaracharya of Kamakoti] faithful, competent, and brilliant disciple, it is being expounded through books and articles with great accuracy and authoritativeness. (15-1-19)

Atman: It is an unconscious handicap to all who have investigated ancient Indian wisdom that they have taken one of its key words, *Atman*, invariably in the terms of our European term "Self." Every Sanskrit scholar conning his texts in some Western university, as every Indian pundit conning them with his foreign pupil, translates this word precisely the same way. The term is currently used in the sense of self in India, but the conception of self to which it is applied bears no comparison with that principle of individual life which is referred to by our Western use of the word. It is a misfortune that having no equivalent to *Atman* among English words, our scholars lazily took the nearest to it instead of going to the trouble of coining an appropriate term as scientists coin new terms every year to fit their new discoveries. For the full implication of *Atman* is wholly ultra-individual and in no way commensurate with self as we use the term. The consequence of this mistranslation has been an immense barrier to right comprehension amongst all Westerners who have grappled with this doctrine. (15-2-278)

Brahman: The Indians have written the most important philosophic statement of all—"All is Brahman"—which I have transposed, possibly to their frowns, as "All is Mind." But one cannot go on repeating it all the time. There are other statements which need to be made, less important but still much to the point for us who have to live in the twentieth century. (12-2-14)

Gnana Yoga: The philosopher will be a *karma yogi* to the extent that he will work incessantly for the service of humanity and work, too, in a disinterested spirit. He will be a *bhakti yogi* to the extent that he will seek lovingly to feel the constant presence of the Divine. He will be a *raja yogi* to the extent that he will hold his mind free from the world fetters but pinned to the holy task he has undertaken. He will be a *gnana yogi* to the extent that he will apply his reflective and reasoning power to a metaphysical understanding of the world. (20-5-18)

Ishvara: The highest object of worship, devotion, reverence—what the Hindus name *Bhakti*—is that which is given to the World-Mind—what Hindus call *Ishvara*. But remember always that you are present within It and It is ever present within you. So the source of grace is in you too. Silence the ego, be still, and glimpse the fact that grace is the response to devotion that goes deep enough to approach the stillness, is sincere enough to put ego aside. Help is no farther off than your own heart. Hope on! (18-5-234)

Maya: The world does exist, we are surrounded by it, and usually we apply the term to something that does not exist. It will be more correct to translate the term *Maya* not by "unreal" but by "not what we think it to be." We must not deny the existence of the world—that would be lunacy—but we must try to get a correct understanding of its hidden nature. (19-1-26)

Mind: There has been so much friction and clash between the different religions because of this idea: whether God is personal or impersonal—so much persecution, even hatred, so unnecessarily. I say unnecessarily because the difference between the two conceptions is only an apparent one. Mind is the source of all; this is Mind inactive. Mind as World-Mind-in-manifestation is the personal God. Between essence and manifestation the only difference is that essence is hidden and manifestation is known. World-Mind is personal (in the sense of being what the Hindus call "Ishvara"); Mind is totally impersonal. Basically, the two are one.   (27-3-56)

Nirvikalpa Samadhi: It is said that in *nirvikalpa samadhi* time is brought to a standstill. Obviously this can only happen when the ego is temporarily paralysed. Ramana Maharshi used to say that the ego is nothing but a bundle of thoughts and does not exist by itself as a separate entity. Nirvikalpa, being the thought-free state and involving the suspension of the movement of thought, is therefore the suspension of the movement of time in the ego's consciousness.   (8-4-470)

Overself: That element in his consciousness which enables him to understand that he exists, which causes him to pronounce the words, "I Am," is the spiritual element, here called Overself. It is really his basic self for the three activities of thinking feeling and willing are derived from it, are ripples spreading out of it, are attributes and functions which belong to it. But as we ordinarily think feel and act, these activities do not express the Overself because they are under the control of a different entity, the personal ego.   (8-1-1)

Sahaja Samadhi: Sahaja samadhi is the awareness of Awareness, whether appearing as thoughts or not, whether accompanied by bodily activities or not. But *nirvikalpa samadhi* is solely the awareness of Awareness. (25-2-140)

Savikalpa Samadhi: It is however a rare occurrence for thought to be utterly stopped, for that state is equivalent to what the Hindus call nirvikalpa samadhi. They have another state, not so far gone, which they call savikalpa samadhi, where thoughts subsist inside the mystic experience and the thinking goes on but is held, so to speak, by the higher experience.

(excerpted from 8-1-221)

Self-absorption: Philosophy stands aligned with mysticism so far as this aim of achieving the profoundest inward self-absorption through meditation is in question, but it stands aloof from mysticism so far as rational, moral, practical, and social issues are in question. A correct appraisal of mysticism can only be formed by examining its ideology against the wider background of philosophic doctrine. (20-4-38)

World-Idea: The World-Idea contains the pattern, intention, direction, and purpose of the cosmos in a single unified thought of the World-Mind. Human understanding is too cramped and too finite to comprehend how this miraculous simultaneity is possible. (26-1-87)

World-Mind: The World-Mind brings our universe into being and governs it, too. The enormous number of objects and creatures which appear through Its agency, through Its power and wisdom, cannot be limited to what is visible alone, and must fill a thinking person with wonder at all the possibilities—a wonder which Plato said must be the beginning of philosophy. (27-2-2)

The Complete Works of Paul Brunton

Early Publications

A Search in Secret India

The Secret Path

A Search in Secret Egypt

A Message from Arunachala

A Hermit in the Himalayas

The Quest of the Overself

The Inner Reality (Discover Yourself)

Indian Philosophy and Modern Culture

The Hidden Teaching Beyond Yoga

The Wisdom of the Overself

The Spiritual Crisis of Man

Published Posthumously

The Notebooks of Paul Brunton

Volume 1: Perspectives

Volume 2: The Quest

Volume 3: Practices for the Quest; Relax and Retreat

Volume 4: Meditation; The Body

Volume 5: Emotions and Ethics; The Intellect

Volume 6: The Ego; From Birth to Rebirth

Volume 7: Healing of the Self; The Negatives

Volume 8: Reflections on My Life and Writings

Volume 9: Human Experience; The Arts in Culture

Volume 10: The Orient

Volume 11: The Sensitives

Volume 12: The Religious Urge; The Reverential Life

Volume 13: Relativity, Philosophy, and Mind

Volume 14: Inspiration and the Overself

Volume 15: Advanced Contemplation; The Peace Within You

Volume 16: Enlightened Mind, Divine Mind

Instructions for Spiritual Living

Paul Brunton: Essential Readings

Meditations for People in Charge

Meditations for People in Crisis

What Is Karma?

The Gift of Grace

The Short Path to Enlightenment

"A person of rare intelligence . . . thoroughly alive, and whole in the most significant, 'holy' sense of the word."

—*Yoga Journal*

"This work, *The Short Path,* consists of meaningful fresh passages that could have been composed today. Brunton was a literary force. His books were better written than those by any of the current communicators of nondual consciousness."

—Jerry Katz, Nonduality.org

"Reading *The Short Path to Enlightenment* was a breath of fresh air to me. Co-editor Jeff Cox has laid out these particular teachings by Paul Brunton in a clear, open and flowing manner. For me, it was the right book at the right time. It helped me to understand my path and where I am on it. The Long Path being the preparation to the Short Path and the role of Grace. Surely, one of the best books on Enlightenment I have read."

—Gary Goldberg, "In the Spirit" radio show, Troy, NY

". . . As Brunton makes clear, the Long Path is necessary preparation for the Short Path, although to some extent both may be undertaken together. His brief, pithy passages present a virtual road map to Self-Realization: concise, practical, no-nonsense, yet very kind, wise and high. Readers will be helped to discover where they are on their own path, and how to move on. Enlightenment is always "immediate" when it happens; here is some solid guidance on diving into the ocean of Grace.

—*Light of Consciousness* magazine

"Any serious man or woman in search of spiritual ideas will find a surprising challenge and an authentic source of inspiration and intellectual nourishment in the writings of Paul Brunton."

—Jacob Needleman